*Life Lit by Some Large Vision*

# LIFE LIT *by* SOME LARGE VISION

*Selected Speeches and Writings*

## Ossie Davis

WITH EDITORIAL NOTES AND A FOREWORD BY

### Ruby Dee

**ATRIA** BOOKS

NEW YORK LONDON TORONTO SYDNEY

**ATRIA** BOOKS
1230 Avenue of the Americas
New York, NY 10020

Library of Congress Cataloging-in-Publication Data

Davis, Ossie
    Life lit by some large vision : selected speeches and writings / Ossie Davis ; with
editorial notes and a foreword by Ruby Dee.
    p. cm.
    I. Dee, Ruby. II. Title.
PS3507.A7444A6 2006
815'.54—dc22

2006040575

ISBN-13: 978-0-7432-8989-4


First Atria Books hardcover edition September 2006

10   9   8   7   6   5   4   3   2   1

**ATRIA** BOOKS is a trademark of Simon & Schuster, Inc.

*Design by Dana Sloan*

Manufactured in the United States of America

For information regarding special discounts for bulk purchases,
please contact Simon & Schuster Special Sales at 1-800-456-6798
or business@simonandschuster.com.

*To my children and grandchildren*

AND

*To all those who may wonder at some future date
just what we were thinking "back in the day."*

*I believe in the training of children black even as white; the leading out of little souls into the green pastures and beside the still waters, not for pelf or peace, but for Life lit by some large vision of beauty and goodness and truth; lest we forget, and the sons of the fathers, like Esau, for mere meat barter their birthright in a mighty nation.*

—W.E.B. Du Bois

# CONTENTS

# ACKNOWLEDGMENTS

In the early 1950s when Ossie and I first began appearing on platforms around the country, we included in our offerings some of the poetry, stories, anecdotes, and philosophies of authors we admired. Chief among those we most always included was Dr. William Edward Burghardt Du Bois. He had been one of my mother's teachers at Atlanta University; had come to see Ossie's play, *Purlie Victorious;* had visited us in our home; and had, with Esther and James Jackson, founded *Freedomways* magazine. He had also been the founder and editor of *The Crisis,* the magazine of the NAACP. Dr. Du Bois deeply affected our personal and world consciousness and summed up, to a large extent, what we wanted our lives to be about.

Thanks to our many friends—known and unknown—who ushered us through this past year. How wonderful to have had this project to help us all move on. Prayers of thanksgiving, dances of praise to:

Nora Davis Day, without whose midwifery this project might have remained in boxes.

Arminda Thomas for months of reading, listening, transcribing, discussing, shaping, and reshaping the manuscript to reflect both Ossie's true voice and my vision. We couldn't have done it without you!

Hasna Muhammad for the contribution of your poem and for your eyes on the manuscript. "Thanks, Doc" from Daddy and me.

Malaika Adero, our editor at Atria/Simon & Schuster, for your belief in and enthusiasm for this project, and to Krishan Trotman for your invaluable assistance. And kudos to Jackie Rebisz for the copyediting.

Susan Crawford, our literary agent, for taking the idea and running with it.

Esther Jackson and Grace Boggs, *cum laude* thanks for the last-minute historical perspective.

Latifah Martin and Rahim Salahuddin—our staff at the office and at home, thanks for keeping the fires burning. Thanks and best wishes to Deborah McGee for her early contributions.

We are particularly thankful to all those who, over the years, contributed tapes, articles, news clips, transcripts, remembrances of Ossie's speeches, talks, and interviews.

And of course, thanks to Ossie—wherever your presence now abides. See, I told you I was going to put you in your *own* book!

# FOREWORD

When Ossie and I first got married, I thought I'd impress him with my respect for order in the universe as well as for the intricate lines and squares and diamond shapes in the argyle socks I was making to caress his feet. Knit. Purl. Knit. Purl. Alas, my handiwork earned me a lukewarm "Oh, Baby, thanks." Not to be deterred from my bridey zeal, I was determined to find a new incentive for my passionate needlework. Knit. Purl. Knit. Purl. Socks just wasn't it.

Mind looking now for some other place to land, to meditate on new ways to make him realize just what a lucky man he was to have me, after all. It was in such moments that I decided to let the world know that my husband, Ossie Davis, was a genius (he had married me, hadn't he?).

I had long known how much Ossie delighted in language—the rhythms in the Bible, for example. He'd often roll out verses in iambic pentameter or some other pattern. He had written poems before we met. I thought they were fascinating, and I soon began sending his poetry to various publications, without success. (Truth be told, only two people ever answered me.)

He treated words as if they tasted good, often laughing out loud at some juxtaposition that hopped into his head or that he'd read or written. I began to witness the spell he cast on audiences, even then, as his brilliance spilled from his brain onto his tongue or from his number 2 pencil, and out into the world. No subject seemed out of his range—it didn't take much to launch him into an encyclopedic treatise on everything from international "isms" to how to get a mule moving or thump a watermelon. He had the wonderful ability to take big ideas and break them down into bite-sized notions, making the complex available, even funny.

Over the years, I gathered up tapes, eulogies, letters, articles—some born of conversations or arguments or time spent around the dinner table with the children. His address at the first Congressional Black Caucus dinner was just such a collaboration. He wondered aloud, one night, what he might say to a group of black politicians that they hadn't already heard. All the children, mouths full, started ad-libbing. I was too busy between the table and the stove to pay much attention. I heard one of them say, "It's not the man; it's the plan, Daddy," countered by "It's not the rap; it's the map." We all howled! From that family brainstorm, Ossie went on to deliver one of the best remembered of his keynote speeches.

He often quoted freely from a number of philosophers of whom he was an avid reader: Schopenhauer, Du Bois, Nietzsche, etc. Later, he gave up quoting from his favorites, saying that he realized that he was just searching in their brains, seeking a way to untangle himself from the chains of racism and other madnesses.

Ossie was a true student of life who never tired of learning. He drew from people, stories, laughing, loving—a fertile environment where he cultivated the ideas that governed his passionate, principled, generous life. This book is the harvest of some of the words he left us.

—RUBY DEE

# SPEECHES

*I have never looked upon myself as a magician. I was not sent by the Almighty to solve all the problems of the world at one fell swoop. I'm not morally arrogant; I accept the fact that maybe this generation was not the one designed by fate to bring peace to the world. But I also believe that it is necessary to stay on the march, to be on the journey, to work for peace wherever we are at all times because the liberty we cherish, which we would share with the world, demands eternal vigilance. And democracy is no easy path, but those of us who believe in it must be prepared to sacrifice in its cause more willingly than those who are prepared to die in wars of aggression. We, too, must be dedicated to the cause of freedom.*

—DURING THE EVENING OF RESISTANCE,
RIVERSIDE CHURCH,
NEW YORK CITY, MARCH 27, 2003

# ADDRESS AT THE PALM GARDEN

～

*October 10, 1952*
*(Originally distributed by the National Council*
*of the Arts, Sciences and Professions)*

R.D.: *No doubt about it! It was not the best of times—*
*especially for white America. Black America already knew about*
*witch hunts, about what happens to troublemakers wanting to vote—*
*lynching, castration, job discrimination. Say what? Communism?*
*Socialism? Liberalism? Are you now or have you ever been . . . ?*
*Weren't you one of those at a meeting on . . . ? Isn't this your picture*
*published in . . . ? People fired. Dying. Broke. Running. Lying.*
*Being brave. Selling out. Betrayal. It was definitely one of the worst*
*of times.*

It is my honor and my privilege to be with you tonight in
this meeting of protest. The inquisition is upon us, and our
very right to meet together and talk like this is under fire. All
over the country, men and women are becoming increasingly
aware of what is happening to their freedom. Teachers of
many years of service are fired without hearings. Actors are
barred from employment because they refuse to be bullied
about their politics. Lawyers, doctors, miners, longshoremen,
newsmen, and publishers are all being violently pushed
around in the grossest violation of civil rights in the history of
the Republic. But, thank God, they are fighting back. The

McCarran Committee has not found itself welcomed every-where. Men are beginning to remember what liberty means to them and have not hesitated, in some places, to drive the witch hunter from their midst. We here tonight can take courage from all the various groups and individuals who have had the guts to put the boot to this evil thing. They have shown that it can be fought. And it must be fought—with every weapon an aroused democracy can lay its hands upon.

I wrote a play called *Alice in Wonder,* which we presented briefly—all too briefly—up in Harlem a week or so ago. And on the basis of that I was invited to come here tonight and speak to you. It wasn't much, this play, but it was mine. And it gave my wife, Miss Ruby Dee—whom I consider the poten-tial equal of any actress in the land—a chance to practice her craft. Few Negroes get that opportunity these days. "Black Channels," you know— For I must tell you that economic in-terdiction (which means that nobody will hire you, no matter how good you are) is not a new thing to us. Negro teachers have long been the victims of the most arrant job discrimina-tion in this city. And Negro actors who work once every five years are doing pretty well. I myself have been lucky—in six years I have managed to work in eight shows on Broadway; and five times out of that eight I carried a tray. I had to. There was nothing else for black performers to carry. Oh yes, I have heard of *Red Channels,** and I am horrified every time I see it

---

*\*Red Channels* (1950) was a pamphlet that listed the names of 151 writers, directors, and performers, and the "subversive" organizations with which they were affiliated. Those individuals were blacklisted in Hollywood. "Black Channels" is a rhetorical play on *Red Channels.*

in action. That a man should be banished from his profession without recourse, merely as a consequence of the color of his politics, is as grossly unjust as that a man should suffer the same punishment merely as a consequence of the color of his face. Red Channels or Black Channels—there's precious little difference to a man with a family to feed. Both these evil things attack me through my need for security, and I cannot hate the one without detesting the other. The good citizen is at war with both!

But back to *Alice in Wonder.* In it, I tried to show two things: first, how absolutely heartbreaking it is to ask a man to give up his bread for his principles; and second, how absolutely necessary it is that he should do just that. For the true function of drama is to remind us that man is dedicated to the pursuit of the good, in spite of himself, and that to pursue the good successfully, he must know the alternatives and choose wisely from among them.

The man I wrote about found himself in a predicament increasingly familiar to us all: he had either to hunt with the hounds of McCarthy and McCarran, or to run with the hares and the victims: the harassed, the persecuted, the falsely stigmatized. To sacrifice his honor in order to keep his job—or have no job to keep. This is indeed a bitter choice. The man I wrote about made one decision. His wife, who loved him dearly, made another. They went their separate ways, and the play was ended.

But for us the curtain is still up. The crisis is at hand, the villain waits in the wings, his cue has been sounded, he makes his entrance—Senator McCarran has come. And to what end, we know only too well. The day is almost gone when any actor could get a job, or any teacher hold one, provided he had the talent and the training; when any playwright, no matter how controversial or nonconforming, could find some producer to put on his works; when any play, however dissenting, had a fair chance to find its audience—uncensored and unencumbered. Now the investigator is kind; controversy gives way to conformity; the rest is silence. The inquisitorial nose has found the theater a fleshpot of liberal ideas and practices, a cesspool of light and of joy, the one place on our national scene where democracy was close to coming alive. Such an aura of high spirits, such an atmosphere of universal goodwill was hardly conducive to the hunting of witches. It had to be destroyed. From now on, Senator McCarran proposes to write the dialogue.

It has been said of the theater that it is vain, that it is foolish, that it is trivial. That it has nothing of consequence to say, that it is no longer the conscience of the nation, that it does not concern itself with the bitter realities of life, that it has cut itself off from its roots in the masses, that it has become the self-indulgent vocal cords of privilege. All too often these charges have been justified.

But, is this all? Is this the picture completely? Is this the whole story? No! There have been giants among us, and few as they have been, they have left a heritage worth defending. The theater is not dead. It is very much alive. And we must keep it alive because we need it now more than ever. There is hope to be fetched, and faith to be carried. There is the problem to be defined, the strength to be mobilized, a conscience to be aroused, an enemy to be defeated. The theater has work to do. The great witch hunter is upon us. He is formidable. He is evil, but he can be stopped. He must be stopped, and together we can do the job. The future of the meaning of America is being decided, and I call upon each of us here tonight to put his hand into the making of that decision. The issue is simple: to surrender the most precious item in our democratic store-house—the Bill of Rights—into the hands of its despisers; or to turn and defend it with all the force and fire at our command. There is but one course left consistent with honor, dignity, and human decency. Free men will always fight!

# THE ENGLISH LANGUAGE IS
# MY ENEMY

~

*"Racism in Education" Conference of the*
*American Federation of Teachers*
*December 1966*

R.D.: *I could feel the horn popping through my right temple. "You mean the whole English language—enemy?"*

*"Oh come on, Ruby," he said. "You know I'm just talking about how English is often complicit in sanctioning racism."*

*"Every language is guilty of that, I bet. What language you suggest we come up with?" I smarted.*

*Razor to his chin, he said, "Score one for Shorty, Lord help me."*

O.D.: *Ruby still thinks I was a little too hard on the mother tongue. I didn't, and I don't. I still don't turn my back on an open dictionary.*

I stand before you a little nervous, afflicted to some degree with stage fright. Not because I fear you, but because I fear the subject.

The title of my address is "Racism in America—Broad Perspectives of the Problem," or "The English Language Is My Enemy."

In my speech I will define culture as the sum total of ways of living built up by a group of human beings and transmitted by one generation to another. I will define education as the act or process of imparting and communicating a culture, developing the powers of reasoning and judgment, and generally preparing oneself and others intellectually for a mature life.

I will define communication as the primary means by which the process of education is carried out.

I will say that language is the primary medium of communication in the educational process and, in this case, it is the English language. I will indict the English language as one of the prime carriers of racism from one person to another in our society and discuss how the teacher and the student, especially the Negro student, are affected by this fact.

The English language is my enemy.

Racism is a belief that human races have distinctive characteristics, usually involving the idea that one's own race is superior and has a right to rule others. Racism.

The English language is my enemy.

But that was not my original topic—I said that English was my goddamn enemy. Now why do I use "goddamn" to illustrate this aspect of the English language? Because I want to illustrate the sheer gut power of words. Words which control our action. Words like "nigger," "kike," "sheeny," "dago," "black power"—words we don't use in ordinary decent conversation, one to the other. I choose these words deliberately, not to flaunt my freedom before you. If you are a normal human being, these words will have assaulted your senses: your pulse rate is possibly higher, your breath quicker; there is perhaps a tremor along the nerves of your arms and your legs; sweat begins in the palms of your hands, perhaps. With these few words

I have assaulted you. I have damaged you, and there is nothing you can possibly, possibly do to control your reactions—to defend yourself against the brute force of these words.

These words have a power over us; a power that we cannot resist. For a moment, you and I have had our deepest physical reactions controlled, not by our own wills, but by words in the English language.

A superficial examination of Roget's thesaurus of the English language reveals the following facts: The word "whiteness" has 134 synonyms, 44 of which are favorable and pleasing to contemplate, for example: "purity," "cleanness," "immaculateness," "bright," "shiny," "ivory," "fair," "blonde," "stainless," "clean," "clear," "chaste," "unblemished," "unsullied," "innocent," "honorable," "upright," "just," "straightforward," "fair," "genuine," "trustworthy," and only 10 synonyms of which I feel to be negative—and then only in the mildest sense—such as "gloss over," "whitewash," "gray," "wan," "pale," "ashen," etc.

The word "blackness" has 120 synonyms, 60 of which are distinctly unfavorable, and none of them even mildly positive. Among the offending 60 were such words as "blot," "blotch," "smut," "smudge," "sullied," "begrime," "soot," "becloud," "obscure," "dingy," "murky," "low-toned," "threatening," "frowning," "foreboding," "forbidding," "sinister," "baneful," "dismal," "thundery," "wicked," "malignant," "deadly," "unclean," "dirty," "unwashed," "foul," etc. In addition, and this is what really hurts, 20 of those words—I exclude the villainous 60 above—are related directly to race, such as "Negro," "Negress," "nigger," "darkey," "blackamoor," etc.

If you consider the fact that thinking itself is subvocal

speech (in other words, one must use words in order to think at all), you will appreciate the enormous trap of racial prejudgment that works on any child who is born into the English language.

Any creature, good or bad, white or black, Jew or Gentile, who uses the English language for the purposes of communication is willing to force the Negro child into 60 ways to despise himself, and the white child, 60 ways to aid and abet him in the crime.

Language is a means of communication. This corruption, this evil of racism, doesn't affect only one group. It doesn't take white to make a person a racist. Blacks also become inverted racists in the process.

A part of our function, therefore, as teachers will be to reconstruct the English language. A sizable undertaking, but one which we must undertake if we are to cure the problems of racism in our society.

The English language must become democratic. It must become respectful of the possibilities of the human spirit. Racism is not only reflected in words relating to the color of Negroes. If you will examine some of the synonyms for the word "Jew," you will find that the adjectives and the verb of the word "Jew" are offensive. However, if you look at the word "Hebrew" you will see that there are no offensive connotations to the word.

When you understand and contemplate the small differences between the meanings of one word supposedly representing one fact, you will understand the power—good or evil—associated with the language. You will understand also why there is a tremendous fight among the Negro people to stop using the word "Negro" altogether and substitute "Afro-American."

You will understand even further, how men like Stokely Carmichael and Floyd McKissick can get us in such serious trouble by using two words together: "Black Power." If Mr. McKissick and Mr. Carmichael had thought a moment and said "Colored Power," there would have been no problem.

We come today to talk about education. Education is the only valid transmitter of American values from one generation to another. Churches have been used from time immemorial to teach certain values to certain people, but in America, as in no other country, it is the school that bears the burden of teaching young Americans to be Americans.

Schools define the meaning of such concepts as success. And education is a way out of the heritage of poverty for Negro people. It's the way we can get jobs.

Education is that which opens that golden door that was so precious to Emma Lazarus. But education in the past has basically been built on the theory that we could find those gifted individuals among the Negro people and educate them out of their poverty, out of their restricted conditions; and then, they would, in turn, serve to represent the best interests of the race. If we concentrated on educating Negroes as individuals, we would solve the problem of discrimination by educating individual Negroes out of the problem.

But I submit that that is a false and erroneous function and definition of education. We can no longer, as teachers, concentrate on finding the gifted black child in the slums—or in the middle-class areas—and giving him the best that we have. This no longer serves the true function of education, if education indeed is to fulfill its mission to assist and perpetuate the drive of the Negro community to come into the larger American society on the same terms as all other communities have come.

Let us look for a brief moment at an article appearing in *Commentary* in February 1964, written by the associate director of the American Jewish Committee.

What is now perceived as the "revolt of the Negro" amounts to this [he says]. The solitary Negro seeking admission into the white world through unusual achievement has been replaced by the organized Negro insisting upon a legitimate share for his group of the goods of American society. The white liberal, in turn, who whether or not he is fully conscious of it, has generally conceived of progress in race relations as the one-by-one assimilation of deserving Negroes into the larger society, now finds himself confused and threatened by suddenly having to come to terms with an aggressive Negro community that wishes to enter en masse.

Accordingly, in the arena of civil rights, the Negro revolution has tended to take the struggle out of the courts and bring it to the streets and the negotiating tables. Granting the potential for unprecedented violence that exists here, it must also be borne in mind that what the Negro people are now beginning to do, other ethnic minorities who brought to America their strong traditions of communal solidarity did before them. With this powerful asset, the Irish rapidly acquired political strength and the Jews succeeded in raising virtually an entire immigrant population into the middle class within a span of two generations. Viewed in this perspective, the Negroes are merely the last of America's significant ethnic minorities to achieve communal solidarity and to grasp the role of the informal group power structure in protecting the rights and advancing the opportunities of the individual members of the community.

Liberal opinion in the North and in the South thus continues to stand upon its traditions of gradualism—that of one-by-one admission of deserving Negroes into the larger society and rejection of the idea that to help the Negro it must help first the Negro community.

In the American pattern, where social power is distributed by groups, the Negro has come to recognize that he can achieve equal opportunities only through concerted action of the Negro community. We can't do it one by one anymore; we must do it as a group.

Now, how is education related to the process not of lifting individuals but of lifting a whole group by its bootstraps and helping it climb to its rightful place in American society?

One of the ways is by calling such meetings as this to discuss Negro history—to discuss those aspects of Negro culture which are important for the survival of the Negro people as a community. There is nothing in the survival of the Negro people as a community that is inherently hostile to the survival of the interests of any other group.

When we say "Black Power" and "Black Nationalism," we

do not mean that that is the only power or that that is the only nationalism that we are concerned about or that it is to predominate above all others. We merely mean that it should have the right of all other groups and be respected as such in the American way of life.

Teachers have a very important function. They have before them the raw materials of the future. And if we were satisfied by the job that was being done in our country and in our culture it would not be necessary to call a protest conference. It would be necessary only to call a conference to celebrate.

I submit that racism is inherent in the English language because the language is an historic expression of the experience of a people; that racism, which is the belief that one group is superior to the other and has the right to set the standards for the other, is still one of the main spiritual policies of our country as expressed in the educational process.

Those of us who are concerned, those of us who are caught up, those of us who really want to be involved, must be prepared at this conference to tear aside our most private thoughts and prejudices, remembering that we have been taught them because we are all born to the English language.

Let us not feel personally guilty or personally responsible for the fact that we may not like Negroes. Let us remember that we are participating in the culture which has taught us not to like them, so that, when we are tempted to teach a child from above his position, or to say that "I represent white Anglo-Saxon gentility and culture, and out of the gratitude and graciousness of my heart I am going to reach down and lift you up to my level," we know that is the incorrect attitude.

We cannot reach down and lift up anymore, we must all get down together and reciprocate one to the other and come up together.

Let us, above all, be honest one with the other. Let us pursue truth though it hurts, though it makes us bleed. I said in the beginning that my purpose in using those lacerating words was to expose our innermost feeling. We must dig even deeper for the roots in our own consciousness, black and white, of the real fact of racism in our culture, and having faced that in ourselves, go back to the various schools from which we came and look upon the children before us as an opportunity, not only to practice the craft of teaching and the imparting of knowledge but, equally important, as an opportunity to learn from a subjugated people its value, its history, its culture, its wealth as an independent people. Let there be in our classrooms a sharing of the wealth of American democracy.

I have had occasion (and with this I'll come to a close) to function as a teacher. I'm a bootleg teacher: I teach Sunday school—it's the closest I can get to the process. I teach boys from nine to twelve, and I have the same problem with getting them to appreciate the spoken and written word as you do, in your daily classrooms. Most of them can't read. I don't see how they're going to get not only to Heaven, I don't see how they're going to get to the next grade unless they can conquer some of these problems.

But, more importantly, I am also involved in the educational process. And those of us who are involved in culture and cultural activities do ourselves and our country a great injustice not to recognize that we, too, are communicators and

have, therefore, a responsibility in the process of communication. I could be hired today to communicate to the American
public my great delight in smoking a cigarette, but I know
that a cigarette could cause you cancer. I could be used to do
many other things in the process of communication from the
top to the bottom.

I have a responsibility to show that what I do, what is translated through me, is measured by the best interest of my country, my people, and my profession. And in that I think we are
all together.

# ON THE ASSASSINATION
# OF MARTIN LUTHER KING, JR.

*Central Park, April 5, 1968*

R.D.: *We were still stinging from Malcolm's assassination when, on the night of April 4, 1968, the news came across our television screen: Martin Luther King, Jr., dead in Memphis. Ossie and I—and millions of others—added his name to the roll: the list of the many who had risen up to take a stand and been cut down. Once again, America kills its black heroes. We often mapped strategy and daydreamed aloud of a "bodyguard committee" to protect and defend our leaders, to save them from the fate of being shot down like dogs or bombed or beaten to death. How, then, to dry our eyes yet again, and pick up the torch?*

Brothers and sisters, we gather at this spot in Central Park to make a statement of expression of how we feel about the world as it stands before us. A great man has fallen, and the world waits for our response. The fact that he was an apostle of love and nonviolence might have led many in the world to mistake his personal courage as a man, but nobody who listened to the last words he said on the night before he was slain can doubt that Martin Luther King was one of the bravest black men we have lost in the struggle.

Martin King left us not only the example of his life and of

his thoughts and his philosophies and his teaching, but—this is more important to the young people in our country, to the black people in our country—he left us the example of his death. He knew it was coming, and he didn't run, he didn't change, he didn't back down. He went forward and he met it like a black man always meets it.

Now why was Martin Luther King in Memphis? Was he there just preaching sermons? No. Was he there holding a seminar on nonviolence? No. He was not there delivering a lecture or receiving a Nobel Prize from the high powers of the world. He went to Memphis to help his black deprived brothers win their bargaining rights from the city of Memphis, and we have got to go and see that they give it to them.

They talk to us about what kind of people we are. They laugh at us because we have to feed our families from what we can get on welfare. They say to us, "Why do you ask the government to do so much for you and the government hasn't done anything for anybody else?" They say that we love welfare, that we are not men, that we don't care for our wives and our children, that we don't want to work. In Memphis, men are trying to work, trying to earn enough to send their kids to school, to put bread on their tables, and you killed a man. How much? How much, America, do you expect us to bear? There is no time left.

When we had another brother who stood up for his people, he was gunned down in February of 1965, Malcolm X. Just before Malcolm died, he went down to Selma, where Martin Luther King was having some trouble, and Malcolm went to offer him his hand in friendship. And Malcolm said, "We may differ, Martin King, on tactics. We may differ on philosophy. We may differ on many things. But you are black, and I am black, and let's not forget that. And let's stand together on that basis." And isn't it prophetic that just a few weeks ago, Martin Luther King—Nobel Prize winner, big man in the world, popular with black folks, popular with white folks, Martin Luther King—went to Newark and visited LeRoi Jones and made the same brotherhood statement that Malcolm had made to him: "The fact that we are black is enough to establish our unity and the basis of our fight in this country."

My wife and I are looking forward to being in Memphis on Monday to carry forward the march that Dr. King was going to . . . I don't know . . . Dr. King's body is back in Atlanta. The leaders are having a meeting, deciding what is to be done, so I don't know what the circumstances are. I do know there will be a march, and I do know that I want to be in that number, and I would like to feel that those of you who stand here, black and white—shamed, insulted, spat in the face of your manhood and your dignity and your belief in democracy by that stupid fool and his bullet in Memphis—that you will be there, too. On to Memphis!

Those brothers, those black brothers in Memphis who sent for Martin King, they still need our help. They put up a brave fight, and they lost one of us. But for every Martin they cut down, there must be a hundred Martins to step into his shoes. And as I stand before you, I don't ask whether you are a white Martin or whether you are a black Martin. I ask, first, if you are a man; and second, if you believe that men should stand or fall for freedom; and, third, if you believe that the time for that freedom is now, that you will take those steps now. Now. Now.

Thank you.

# IT'S NOT THE MAN, IT'S THE PLAN

~

*Congressional Black Caucus Dinner*
*June 18, 1971*

O.D.: *Shirley Chisholm thought that I should do the keynote address at the first fundraiser for the Congressional Black Caucus. I wasn't so sure, so I brought it up at the dinner table. You should have heard what Ruby and the children told me! As a matter of fact, you probably did.*

Ladies, gentlemen, brothers, sisters, and friends:
This is an historic occasion, a moment we have dreamed and worked and fought for longer than we ourselves have been alive. The light that kept our fathers and our mothers tuned in to possibilities of a better future when they were slaves—the insights they gleaned, the hopes they hoped, the prayers they prayed—have come one step closer to being answered by what you have collectively done by your presence here tonight.

I have been told that there are 2,800 of us here, and we occupy facilities which were meant for 2,400. That's a pretty good indication of what price we place on our freedom and on the men and women dedicated to fighting for it.

You might have wondered why I, an actor and a performer among other things, was chosen to give the keynote address tonight. And I myself, when called upon to do so, had moments of hesitation and doubt, and I wondered, why choose me for such an important task? I guess the one reason that makes any sense is that I represent that aspect of black culture which began in Africa with the storytellers and came down to the great rhetorical giants who have stirred us with their words in the past.

But I think the time has, perhaps, come when rhetoric will begin to take a backseat. And I was so stirred by that possibility that I decided to give my few remarks a subject, a title, a text I want you to listen to very carefully. The text is very simply: *It's not the man, it's the plan.* And, for those of us who need more explicit information, those of us still caught up in the dreams that rhetoric will solve our problems, let me state it another way: *It's not the rap, it's the map.*

We have been blessed in our past with many great leaders, leaders whose qualifications have been proven by what they did, and what they said—and even by the fact that when the time came they didn't hesitate to give their lives. And their dedication and hard work bears fruition by where we are tonight. I don't call for a moment of silence and gratitude for what the fathers have given us, but we shouldn't go forward without remembering that we are a continuous chain. We celebrate tonight, but we don't celebrate the past; we celebrate the future. And if anybody has a right to celebrate the future, I'm sure we must be that particular people.

We have had great leaders in the past who have stirred us with their words, with their hopes, and with their dreams. I remember coming to Washington in 1963, when Dr. Martin Luther King stood at the Lincoln Memorial and said to the

world, to the Congress, and to the nation, "I have a dream!"
Now, that dream of 1963 was not realized then, it was not
realized at the time of his death, and it has not been realized
now.

At the time when Dr. King died in 1968, he was in the
process of organizing his forces and calling upon his people to
come one more time to Washington, D.C., and I have a feeling that had he come that time, he would not have said, "I
have a dream." He would have said, "I have a plan." And I feel
that that plan he had might have made the difference.

You know, it might do us good to examine some of the
plans our previous leaders have had which actually worked,
and perhaps it is a great misfortune that we never had a chance
to get from them—either individually or collectively—just
what the plan was that they had in mind.

And that's why tonight the burden of my appeal to you—
to the thirteen Congressional Black Caucus members—is to
give us a plan of action. Give to us a "Ten Black Command-
ments," simple and strong, that we can carry in our hearts and
in our memories, no matter where we are, and reach out and
touch and feel the reassurance that there is behind everything
we do a simple, moral, intelligent plan that must be fulfilled in
the course of time. Even if all our leaders, one by one, fall in
the battle, somebody will rise and say, "Our leader died while
we were on page three of a plan; now that the funeral is over,
let us proceed to page four."

You know, what we call for is not without precedent.
When Moses led the children of Israel out of Egypt, they had
to wander around for a long time in the wilderness trying to

get it together. In fact, it took Moses forty years and a stone tablet beating them in the head every day, trying to make Jews out of them. If it took Moses—with God's direct help—forty years, certainly we can give ourselves a few more days to get our thing together. But Moses did have the plan, and Moses took the plan and taught it to the children as best he could.

That's what we need from our leaders now. From our noble thirteen, we need that they think the problems through, investigate possible solutions, codify their results, and present their programs to us—the people—so that we may ratify what they have thought and organized and left to us as a plan of action.

Now we need a plan because we stand at a dangerous but exciting junction of history. We might remind ourselves tonight that we are at a spot where the Irish were some hundred years ago. The Irish had the distinction, of course, of being the "niggers" of their day, and they responded rather angrily and violently to that classification. I don't know if you were around in 1863, but in July of that year, the Irish pitched a dinger in New York which cost the lives of a thousand people. Now, *Life* magazine has given us credit for having created the biggest riot in the U.S., but it forgot that in 1863, there was a riot in New York where over a thousand people died. At that time, the Irish were so embittered by the treatment they received that they blackened their faces, put on women's clothes, went into the mines, and blew them up. They shot people, and they hung people—they did all kinds of bad things. The Molly Maguires wrote a considerable chapter in our history, and not all of it was nonviolent. But the Irish had to learn an additional factor before they were able to walk into the Promised Land, and that factor was that it wasn't enough just to be violent. The Irish had to have a plan. And they had their plan and they got it together in a little town called Boston. They got their thing together. They planned it out, and they said to themselves, "Now look, there's a lot of us Irishmen here in Boston, a whole lot of us, and we've been petitioning the white Anglo-Saxon Protestants for years about better schools and better houses and jobs and the drug problem and the drinking problem and what we're going to do for the future, and we don't get no response from them. So, why don't we Irishmen get together and put our votes into one place and see what we can do if we take power to City Hall."

And do you know, that's exactly what they did. They put their votes together according to the plan, and they came up with one man, the first Irish Catholic mayor of Boston. His name was John Fitzgerald—and you can see where I'm heading because those are the first two names of the first Irish-Catholic president, who was his grandson: John Fitzgerald Kennedy.

Now if it happened to the Irish, who certainly don't represent 25 million people, why can't it happen to us? But the Irish had a plan. They thought it out, and they got all the Irish together, and they said we're going to knock heads and we're going to wield shillelaghs until we get one solid body of Irish opinion. And we might think tonight that we are at that particular juncture; and to some degree we are. We have become hip to the meaning of political power, and that's why we're here. This is an exercise in power tonight. We've eaten a good meal, we've paid good money for it, we've had good fellowship, we've heard good music and entertainment; but, brothers and sisters, the name of the game is power—and if you ain't playing power, you're in the wrong place.

But at this particular juncture in history, the Irish example is not quite enough, because the circumstances in which we live in our society—economically, socially, politically—have qualitatively changed from what they were even twenty years ago. It is that change which makes our fight different and vital, and any plan that we make must take an account of the fact of that particular change that happened in American society. I refer very simply to a very simple but profound phenomenon, which has affected our people more than anybody else.

To make it clear, let me go back in history a little. We came to this country not of our own free will. We came over in the boat as slaves, and we became slaves in the South and in the North; that was our designation and our station. And no matter what you might say against slavery, how much you might abhor it, as an economic system slavery did have one advantage—it had 100 percent job security. When we had the second American Revolution in the 1860s and wiped out slavery, we changed the title of our labor, but we didn't change the constitution of it very much. We stopped being slave labor, but we became cheap labor; and all of the jobs that nobody else wanted to do were ours by right. We had a right to the dirty jobs. Nobody could keep us from cleaning out the john. Nobody stood between us and cooking the grits for Miss Ann in the morning. Nobody stopped our PhD's from hustling baggage down at the Pennsylvania Station. All of the dirty jobs, the hardworking jobs, the unskilled jobs were ours. All of the jobs at the bottom of the pile were ours. And as long as we were content to stay at the bottom, there was a place for us in America—economically, politically, socially, and otherwise. And sometimes when we forgot that place, there was a cadre of Friends of the Black People called the Ku Klux Klan, whose job was to remind us what our place was and to put us back.

But however horrendous that place was, it did offer us some kind of economic purchase in our country. And out of those small jobs that we did have, we could send our children to school. We could build our churches, support our newspapers, and organize our social clubs. It wasn't much, but what little we had did help us keep going as a people.

But a strange thing has happened to the economy of our country, and it's happened very quietly and over a short period. I understand that four years ago, 95 percent of the cotton in Mississippi was picked by machine. We were brought to this country to pick that cotton; we were tied to that cotton culturally, economically, socially, and politically; consider the implications of that fact. Ninety-five percent of the cotton in Mississippi was picked by machines. What happened to those black folks who used to pick that cotton? What became of them? Half of them stayed on the plantation and rotted; the other half came north, and you will find them now in the central cities.

That is the source of one of the problems we face, and this is one of the problems we must solve. Among our people, out of every four jobs in the past, three have been in the classification of unskilled—the rough jobs that required very little education. Those three jobs out of every four are the natural target of the automation and mechanical revolution, by which this country now produces more and more goods every year with the use of less and less manpower. But what I'm trying to tell you is that the black man and woman, the black family, stands directly in the path of automation and the mechanization of our economic life in this country, and this is an irreversible process. The end result of it you see now on the welfare rolls in our cities. In New York, one out of every five citizens is on welfare. Now, you may think that somehow we'll solve the problem and one day eliminate welfare, but I doubt that is true. I think the whole process is one way—that welfare is this society's answer to its economic dislocation, to its endemic unemployment for which it has no solution, nor the determination to find a solution.

If the masses of black people who at least did have a place on the bottom of society now suddenly find that that place is denied us, what recourse have we except what you find already in the inner cities? The fires of rebellion are burning brightly because human beings can only be repressed and ignored and maltreated for so long. Then they must rise. What is the response of the black people in our inner cities to this endemic unemployment? What happens to our youth, who suffer from 25 to 50 percent unemployment? Some of them take to drugs. Some of them take to crime. Some of them apply themselves and say the solution to the problem is education; the solution is preparing ourselves to deal with an automated society, to deal with a computerized economy. There are others who say that the society has no alternative, nothing to give me but a tour of duty in Vietnam. Still others say the only recourse is revolution—to change the society by any means we can before the society decides that because we are expendable and black and poor and dejected and despised that they would rather see us in the ovens of Dachau than solve the problems as rational men.

I do not say that the society is already organized to exterminate black people—by no means. I say that we must from now on begin to consider all possibilities and to prepare for all eventualities ourselves. When the other immigrants came to our society—the Hungarians, the Jews, the Irish, the Germans—they at least had the hard jobs to do: the ditches to dig, the baggage to hustle, the docks to wallop. They could find the hard work, and could make enough with their hard work and their labor, so that their children could climb on their backs into the outer society. If we still had that opportunity, we would do likewise.

But what I'm trying to tell you, ladies and gentlemen, is that those ditches they dug are no longer diggable, that the economy which they fed no longer needs that kind of labor, and that even though we now have on our law books many, many more rules and regulations regarding the freedom of black people, until we can solve the economic problem of how we get around the fact that people do not climb up as groups in American society by digging ditches anymore, we are in serious trouble. Members of the Congressional Black Caucus, you may be called upon to prove once and for all that work is an outmoded commodity in America—that men deserve dignity, and an income, and a definition as valuable citizen whether they have a job or not. It may be that you will have to define work, citizenship, ownership, and property in a totally brand-new light. That may be your assignment. That may be what history requires of you. Brothers and sisters, I repeat: It's not the man, it's the plan!

We've had great leaders and we loved them. We admired them. They brought us where we are. But rhetoric will not do it now. Rapping alone will not make it. What we need from you, our honored leaders—and I choose the word advisedly, our honored leaders—what we need from you are your best thoughts, your sincerest dedication. We need from you a re-assurance that there is a needed political alignment even in the black community now.

We no longer elect our leaders by the value they bring to us, or the good they can bring to us in the white community. We elect leaders who represent what we are and what we can do—and if we can spend a quarter of a million dollars on a dinner, there's a lot that we can do. I think, for instance, that the Black Caucus should have a dinner like this in every major city where blacks are gathered. I think it would be good if they went into the communities as a group to be seen by the people, so that the blacks in all areas, in all cities, can participate as you participate here tonight.

Let me say in closing that though I look at the economic structure of our society and see the unemployment figure creeping higher—so that now even executives face an unemployment rate of six percent—and I know what that means for the black community; though it is dire, though we see drug addiction, we see our inner cities decaying, we see the imminent collapse of much that we've held dear, still, black congressmen, you are not without power, even at this moment.

When you consider that every Monday morning, the preachers in Harlem bank $1.5 million, maybe you black congressmen might tell the preachers, "Brother, it's time for you to put all that money in a black bank somewhere." When you consider that in the course of a year, in my own Harlem community again, $1.1 million will be spent by churches and social organizations on banquet facilities downtown, you may say to them, "Let us build our facility uptown. Let us spend our money among ourselves." And think of this simple little thing: There is one firm in New York that does the printing for the churches on Sunday at the cost of $250,000 a year—one white firm servicing all the black churches, $250,000 leaving the community, never to come back. I think our thirteen congressmen might have some solution as to what we should do about things like that. I, for instance, personally need help with a problem. I directed a motion picture called *Cotton Comes to Harlem,* which has grossed $6.5 million to date. Now, 60 to 70 percent of the money that went across the box office came from black people. Money that came from the Harlems of all our cities, the Harlems of all our country, money that goes to Hollywood, and it's one-way—ain't coming back. I have been instrumental in helping rob—well, not rob exactly—*borrow* from my people money that we need in our own community. I need your help in structuring a way that when the money goes to Hollywood it only stays for a little while; it doubles and comes back to the black community.

Ladies and gentlemen, brothers and sisters, I think I've

said enough. There's much that could be talked about tonight; but we are here, and the fact that we are here is itself eloquent. This is a dinner that could have been served without a single word because we know the historical significance of just sitting, looking, talking to each other of what this moment means. And if you think there are others who don't know what this moment means, you should be somewhere where the listening devices are tuned up very high.

But all I'm saying to the world, all I'm saying to that cadre of black leadership is that we want a plan. We want a plan so simple, so easy to remember that we carry it in our heads. So that if the storm of oppression should wipe us out, all out but one family, and that family was crouching somewhere in the dark, one brother would reach out to another and say, "Hey, hey man, what's the plan?"

Let us stop making history by ad hoc methods and impromptu improvisations. Let us plan the whole thing out, give everybody his assignment, and hold him strictly responsible if he doesn't carry it out. That's what is called for. We are capable of doing it, and now is the time to do just that.

# BE NOT TOO TAME, NEITHER

＊

*Keynote Speech, American Theater Association Convention*
*(Printed in* Dramatics, *June 1983)*

I believe in theatre as one of the most important activities available to man- and womankind. In our society and in the climate of our times, all too often those of us who are practitioners—particularly those of us who do not live in New York, who work in theatres less than profitable—tend to look at ourselves and see somebody small. It is against that image of us as outside operators that I would like to hold forth.

We live in parlous times, in the midst of startling changes coming at us with such rapidity that often we lose our footing. Sometimes so much happens so fast, the temptation is to take the easy way out, to give up on the unending necessity of forcing ourselves to look at our situation, of forcing ourselves to grow, of forcing ourselves to change. Sometimes moral fatigue tends to set in. We grow weary. The doors close in our faces one time too many; the grants are denied or withdrawn; the community gives us the cold shoulder; the actors we would train and employ do not seem to care and spend too much time in the bathroom smoking pot. It is easy under those circumstances to accept a smaller sense of our responsibility. We wind up saying to ourselves, let us just make it from day to day, to the end of the week—pick up the paycheck and go home.

It is at that time, when our resources and our energies are at their lowest, that we need to take a second look at ourselves in terms not only of our responsibilities but also of our opportunities. Our society has the church and it needs the church; our society has the school and it needs the school; but equally important to our minds and our spirits and our souls is the theatre. We must have the courage to think of theatre in those terms.

We must look upon the audience in America not as what they are but as what we expect them to be. We must expect that they grow, we must expect that they expand, we must expect that their tastes will improve. We must take it for granted that the movement is ever upward, and we must conduct our theatrical enterprises with those expectations. The audience tail cannot be allowed to wag the theatrical dog.

But in order for our expectations to be realized, we must first believe in them ourselves. We must believe not only that the theatre is important, and that it has an important function to fulfill, but that it *can* fulfill that function, and that the test of its fulfillment will be an elevation of the common taste in American society. If we haven't got that much chutzpah, we should not be in the theatre. I invite those who fail this test to take up pall bearing or some other service to the dead, because we who are still alive need our spirits quickened; we need our imaginations stimulated; we need our visions lifted. We need the reassurance that beneath it all there are solid, basic principles which endure, even if humankind will not endure. We need to believe that it is essential that we should do right, though the heavens fall.

And this brings me to my text: "Be not too tame, neither." I like that, because if Shakespeare can double up on them negatives, so can I. You remember that speech, of course. It's from Hamlet's instruction to the players. We are, according to the Bard, the mirrors of our times. Let's not take too much comfort in that bit of imagery. It is easy to think of a mirror merely as a passive instrument: he who looks in, looks out; if a fool looks in, a genius will not look out.

Our job, obviously, is to reflect the form and pressures of our times. And we can easily duck our responsibility by picking out those elements of our times which pander to the lowest instincts in humankind. We look abroad, see evidence of depravity, of brutality. We see war and all of its horrors, we catalogue the endless roll of man's inhumanity to man. We may therefore be excused if in our theatres we say our job is to mirror what life is really like. And life is hell. Life is awful. Life, as they say on the street corner, is a bitch. So, if you hear words in the theatre that you are not used to, if you see actions that you haven't seen before, if things there offend your sensibilities, don't blame us, we are merely mirrors of what is abroad in the times.

That excuse will not hold water. That excuse will not sell. The mirror does reflect what it sees; but on looking in the mirror, we also gain instructions about our appearance. If our lipstick is on crooked, the mirror tells us and we make the corrections. The mirror offers us a chance to improve our appearance, an opportunity to follow our best—not our less noble—instincts.

We know from our own experience that men and women are essentially divided characters. We have at the core of our existence a paradox and a contradiction. It is as easy to do evil as it is to do good. As a matter of fact, it is much easier to do evil than to do good. It is as easy to let things slide as it is to assume responsibility for yourself, your family, your nation, and all mankind. It is easy to worship self-fulfillment, the following of personal and private inclinations. What else does freedom mean, but the fact that I walk abroad untrammeled, free to indulge my appetite? Don't touch me, I claim protection under the First Amendment.

We know that is wrong. If we follow purely our inclinations, if we indulge our weaknesses, we do not escape feeling guilty of the consequences. Something within us—and I hold it to be something older, more fundamental than we—gives us direction and moral stamina and courage to follow that direction come what may. We need to tell ourselves that we are indeed strong and that we can become stronger, that there is no ill in our surrounding environment that cannot be addressed and overcome by our intelligence. What is required is our determination that we have in the theatre a high calling. And no matter what the consequences, we remember Lord Hamlet's instructions to the players: we must "be not too tame, neither." We must be brave to follow those things without which a society will not long endure.

Now, it is easy, upon little reflection, to accept the truth in its platitudinous form. It has a good sound, it looks good on a Christmas card, and it's something we can swear to without any fear of contradiction. But think a moment of events that took place in our society in the recent past, events which forced the theatre to look deep within itself, to make decisions and sometimes to stand against the powers that be, putting itself and its practitioners at serious risk.

I remember the fifties, the McCarthyite time, and I remember the marauders who came into the artistic community looking for blood. I remember the deprivations visited upon us in Hollywood and on Broadway. Many distinguished artists were driven abroad from Los Angeles, never to be welcomed again. But those same men and women, refugees as well as returnees, were always able to find a home without quibble in the Broadway theatre. That was what kept that theatre alive. We were involved in an institution and in actions which made us proud of ourselves.

When I came into the theatre, there were many activities in which actors were engaged: fund-raising, propagandizing, rallying to prevent injustice in the far corners of our own country, rallying to make our views known and heard before all the powers. It was a stimulating time to be alive. We were attacked, we were vilified. There were congressional groups that came from Washington to sit in judgment on the theatre, purely because they did not like a resolution passed at an Equity meeting supporting a distinguished actor, Paul Robeson, in his fight to secure a passport.

And even before that time Equity had taken a stand on the issue of segregation in Washington, D.C. It had contractually provided those of us who did not want to play in Washington, because of its segregated theatrical institutions, a way out. It said no member of this union has to play under conditions less than those fit for human decency and brotherhood. I was proud to be associated with a group that was able to take a

stand in direct contradiction to the monetary interests of producers who didn't particularly care what kind of audience we
were playing to as long as the crowds lined up at the box office.

My wife and I, the first year we were married, our collec-
tive gross income was nine hundred dollars. It was not the
bottom of the barrel—we could have survived unemployed
for two or three months longer—but times were tight. We
were asked at that time to take part in a rally that had been
called to protest the coming electrocution of the Rosenbergs, Communist spies. And we didn't have any thoughts
on whether the Rosenbergs were guilty or innocent; we
didn't hold ourselves competent to make that judgment. But
we were glad to associate with other people—scientists,
artists, the pope in Rome himself—in saying to the powers
that be: "This is a mother and father. Whatever their guilt,
do not take their lives. Let them remain alive, particularly
because they are the parents of two children."

Well, this was not an easy thing to say. And those of us
who dared to take that stand could not expect to go unpun-
ished. My wife and I were approached to join that committee,
to rally to the defense of the Rosenbergs—who had, on a
Wheaties box top, given the Russians the secret to the atomic
bomb. We sat down to ponder what we should do. How
might this action affect our future? Should we take such a
stand in view of the jobs that we held? A second's reflection
produced the startling information: What jobs? There we
were, already blacklisted for being black—what would it hurt
if we added a little red and got blacklisted there too?

We decided that we would take the great risk. Ruby, my

wife, went to a rally at Carnegie Hall, and she read poetry among some of the other speakers who were passionate in their defense of our position. In the auditorium that night were two distinguished actors, Howard Da Silva and Morris Carnovsky, who were at that time casting a play that they were going to present Off Broadway, *The World of Sholom Aleichem.* They hired Ruby to do a part, and because there was so little money available, they had a policy that brought me in. They tried to hire two people at a time, so that you could live on one salary and pay your bills with the other, because they knew that what they offered couldn't do the whole job. I came in as a stage manager, and we stayed with *The World of Sholom Alei-chem* for two years.

Because these actors were unemployed, they had to find other means of earning a living. We used to go to union halls, schools, to wherever somebody wanted a work read or drama-tized, and we would do a staged reading of a novel, or some poetry or whatnot, and we would get enough money— Carnovsky, Da Silva, Ruby, myself, and others—to help pay the week's rent. We learned, Ruby and I, that this was a way of being theatrical as well as the other way, and we learned, from Carnovsky and Da Silva, that there was no difference in terms of professional standards and requirements between the actor who merely stood in front of a lectern and the actor who has the benefit of makeup and props and all of the other things. To them, theatre was theatre. And that knowledge was to stand us in good stead, because we were indeed tarred with the same brush that had tarred those distinguished actors, and we found ourselves on some strange and curious lists.

We appeared one summer in a camp, when the state of New York decided that something in the summer camps was creating a threat to the sanity and health and safety of New York State. They launched an investigation, and on one occasion, two men armed with subpoenas descended on the camp and began to hand subpoenas out—to Da Silva, Carnovsky, all of the other performers. We found out that they were looking for us, Ossie Davis and Ruby Dee. But it didn't occur to them that black folks were involved in a theatrical presentation. So they didn't find us. They stayed and watched the night's production. We were doing Chekhov's *The Cherry Orchard.* Ruby had a part and I also had a part, and we went in and out of the production, on and off the stage reciting our lines, while the men with the subpoenas circled around, keeping an eye out for Ruby Dee and Ossie Davis. Once again, they were the victims of their own prejudice—it didn't occur to them that black folks could do anything that merited their attention.

It was only when the curtain was down that it dawned on them that those two black folks were who they were looking for. By that time a young man, the son of J. Edward Bromberg, a distinguished actor who was himself persecuted—and died as a result of it—had given us a way out. Backstage was a huge basket in which we kept all of the costumes that the actors had used for the whole week. The costumes bore the sweat of their ardor, the odor of their activities, and it was a close-knit basket, but we were persuaded to climb into the basket, hide under the funky clothes, and stay there until the minions of the state had come and asked everybody, "Where are Ruby

Dee and Ossie Davis?" Everybody denied that they'd ever heard of two such people, and finally the minions left and we were rescued from the basket. This is an indication of the madness of the time.

But we learned from the experience. What we learned was that there was a possibility of being theatrically effective that had nothing to do with proscenium arches and lights and all of the things that go toward the making of a professional production. We knew that there was also an audience to whom nobody was speaking: a host of black folks who had come from the South with our Southern culture, our Southern poets, and our Southern folktales. We found that if we went to those places where our folks gathered—the churches, the schools, the street corners, union halls, college campuses—and read for our people the things that they loved to hear, they would at least give us enough money to pay our rent and buy food for our children. That was the beginning of our capacity to survive.

And these days, when people salute my wife and me for being brave pioneers—who stood against the assault of the McCarthyites and never lowered their flag, who always stood for principle, who were never afraid to be seen in the company of Paul Robeson and W.E.B. Du Bois, who always spoke their minds and had such an independent attitude toward life—we smile, because what is not understood clearly is that we could afford to be independent. We didn't need to wait for the phone from Hollywood to ring. We didn't even need to wait for the phone from Broadway to ring. Our audience was somewhere else. And they let us know how they felt, both by their thunderous applause and by throwing a couple of bucks into the hat.

There is, in our experience, survival value. There is, in our experience, a growing understanding that American theatre takes place not only on Broadway but all up and down and across this broad land of ours. Those little theatres—those black theatres, those white theatres, those ethnic theatres—which, in spite of all discouragement, grow wheat on bricks and trees out of concrete and stone, set us all a magnificent example. We can grow above and beyond the impossible conditions imposed by our society if we look long enough to understand that *we are the people,* assigned by the Constitution of our country the ultimate responsibility for what happens in our democracy. That there is no officer of our government who is above and beyond our control and our recall. If indeed ours is a government of the people, by the people, and for the people, we the people have got to assume the responsibility.

I admire Mr. Reagan, but only because I think he is an ideologue; I think he is a man of deep beliefs. I oppose all of his basic beliefs, but I too am an ideologue, and I have my own priorities and my own beliefs, and I am as determined to stand up for what I think are human values against the militaristic, deadening materialistic values coming out of Washington, even though it should cost me my comfort and maybe my life, because it is the nature of my commitment that I have to be dedicated to the full. And we all must be dedicated to the full.

Let me close by getting religious.

I believe in God, but I'm not a mystic, and I'm not going

to recommend that you try to resolve all of your problems by prayer. We black folk have been at that for hundreds of years and we haven't made it yet. We know there has to be something besides prayer if you really intend to get things done. Some of us have to dare to believe in moral values and stand up and say that we so believe.

The God inside me needs help. I'm not sure he or she alone can do the job. I interject here a little bit of humor to illustrate my point.

A preacher worked hard many years ago in the vineyards down south and tried to preach brotherhood and was beaten for his pains. He tried to preach Christian responsibility between blacks and whites and was beaten for his pains. Everything he tried to do to make the visions of Jesus Christ come true got him into trouble. Finally he gave up. He quit. He went north. He put it all behind him.

One day, the voice of the Lord spoke to our pastor, saying, "Pastor, you have deserted your responsibilities."

The brother said, "If you know like I know what's going on down there, you would have deserted them, too."

But the Lord responded, "No, my people need you. My people cry for mercy. They cry for shelter. They cry for sustenance. You must go back, back to your responsibilities in the Deep South and preach my gospel."

And the preacher said, "Lord, I've been there. I did all I could. If I go back they'll kill me."

But the Lord insisted. "Even at the cost of all you hold dear, your responsibility is to go back to the South."

Finally the Lord was so eloquent that he persuaded our

pastor to undertake the journey, but he said, "Lord, I am will-ing to go back south, but with this proviso: when I go south, you come with me."

And the Lord pondered a moment, then replied, "I will go with you, my son—as far as Tennessee."

I preach a God who needs our helping hand, who possibly will not make it without us doing something. Those of you who are sitting here in great comfort expecting your God to prevent somebody from dropping that atom bomb on New York City, take another thought. The only God that might do that is the one that sits in you and the one that sits in me. Our responsibility is to open the door and let that God out and fol-low where he or she leads.

# TALKING DRUMS
# AND HAITIAN DUMPLINGS

~

*1995*

R.D.: *Ossie did several versions of this story—sometimes as a stand-alone piece, sometimes as a part of a larger speech. He even worked it into* Two Hah Hahs and a Homeboy, *a three-person show we wrote and performed with our son, Guy. This piece is a compilation of that version and one from a speech he gave in 1991.*

O.D.: *I'm an artist, yes, but really not an actor or even a playwright. I am a storyteller. And this is probably the best that I can do.*

Now, Africa, as you well know, for centuries was a mighty continent on which many of us lived—children of many different heritages, speaking many tongues. The Watusi might live right next door to the Mandingo, or the Swahili to the Ashanti, and not understand a word each other was saying. But that didn't matter: though they might not be able to speak each other's language, they always had in common something they could speak, and that was the talking drum. The drum that sounded from the north to the south, from the east to the west, that brought together all the people on the continent when there was something of great importance that Africans as a whole needed to tend to. For example, it might not have surprised you to come upon the continent one morning when all the drums were sounding on the left, on the right, from the north to the south: *Boom-bada-boom bada boom,* "Everybody duck, here comes Henry Kissinger."

And that's the way it was when slavery came. Millions of our ancestors were captured like prisoners of war, crammed into slave ships, and brought to North America, South America, and to the West Indies, put on the auction block and sold to be worked for nothing on the cotton plantations and the sugar cane plantations.

Some of the biggest and richest sugar cane plantations in the world were in Haiti, which is just east of Cuba, on the island of Hispaniola. That's where, over 250 years ago, the talking drum made history.

Haiti belonged to France, and they had about 25,000 white slaveholders sitting on top of 250,000 black slaves. That's about 10 to 1, and you may ask, why didn't all them slaves rise up, get together, run the slavemasters off and take them plantations for themselves? Well, like I just told you, the different tribes spoke different languages. They couldn't understand each other, and the slavemasters knew it. So whenever they went down to the market to buy a coupla dozen new slaves, they always made sure not to get more than one or two of a kind: two Mandingo, two Herero, two Ashanti, then mix 'em all up together on the same plantation. Two or three hundred slaves, who couldn't understand each other. All they could do was to learn as best they could the language of their masters, which was French. So, when they got together to plot what they were going to do about slavery, to plot how to overthrow the masters and rise up, naturally they had to plot in French. And the masters were smart enough to listen in French, and then they captured them in French. And they hung them in French.

That is, until Toussaint-Louverture came along. Toussaint was strong, Toussaint was brave, Toussaint was ambitious, Toussaint was intelligent, and Toussaint was sick to death of him and his people being slaves. He tried every way he knew how to get the slaves together so they could fight for their freedom, but the people didn't understand a word that he was saying, until he remembered the drums. Then he got some drummers together and told them to send this message to his people: *Rise up, all you black and African people, the time has come to strike a blow for freedom. So put nails in your broomsticks, sharpen your teeth and your toenails, grab your machetes and butcher knives, your Coca-Cola bottles and brickbats . . . Wait for the talking drums to give the signal, then take over the plantations, burn the sugar cane, run the cattle off . . . then don't stop kicking butt till all the slavemasters are gone and we have this whole island for ourselves.*

And you know what happened? They did it. The people heard the drums and came together, like one big black fist, and drove the French slaveholders all the way back to France.

Now, Napoléon Bonaparte was France's man of the hour. He owned almost everything in Europe. He also owned a big hunk of land right here in the United States, right in the center. He owned the city of New Orleans, the Mississippi Valley, the Louisiana Territory. And boy, was he pissed. In the first place, black folks had no right to declare themselves, or anything else, free without first getting permission from somebody white. Second, sugar cane had made it the richest island in the Caribbean; Napoléon needed that money to keep his armies supplied.

So Napoléon called on his brother-in-law Leclerc, who was also a general, and gave him ships, muskets, cannons, and 15,000 of the finest troops in the world. He said, "I want that island back. Go to Haiti, find this Toussaint whatever-his-name-is and kill him, then put those black people back into slavery where they belong!"

When the brothers in Haiti heard that Leclerc was coming, they knew they didn't have the wherewithal to fight against the most modern weapons in society; so they put the torch to the villages and retired into the hills. So when Leclerc's ship skidded to a stop at Port-au-Prince, he jumped out onto the dock, looked all around, but there was nobody there. Only some little half-naked children playing hoops, a few old women with pipes in their mouths and baskets on their heads, and some little old men dressed in white and driving donkeys. Toussaint and his army were nowhere to be found.

"Hey, where's all them bad black folks that were so mean to the white Frenchmen here? We want Toussaint-Louverture, we want Henri Christophe, we want Jean-Jacques Dessalines. Your leaders. Tell them, come here. Leclerc is in town and wants them to come in and surrender."

They say, "Well, sir, they left a long time ago. We don't even know where they are."

So Leclerc said, "All right. We'll stay till they come back."

Leclerc hired the little old ladies smoking their pipes to do the washing, the ironing, and the cooking. Now, for some reason these women didn't cook so well. They would put poison spiders in the dumplings—I mean, who ever heard of such a thing?—and some of the French soldiers would die.

And the little old men, they weren't just little old men driving donkeys; they were also voodoo priests. Now, we don't believe in voodoo here; it doesn't work. But in Haiti, in those days, it actually worked. So, the priests got together and said, "We've been suffering over here in Haiti a long time from yellow fever, them mosquitoes just bite us all the time." So the priests called all the mosquitoes together and said, "Hey, ya'll been sucking black blood ever since we been here, ain't you? You know how runny and thin and strung-out that blood is, 'cause we work so hard?"

"Yeah," the mosquitoes said. "Man, it ain't top-quality blood at all, but it's the best we can do."

The priests said, "Say look, instead of sucking our blood all the time, why don't you suck some of that French blood? Not only is it white, they got champagne mixed all up in it. I tell you what. Why don't you fly over there and pick out one of the fattest ones you can, take him off and drain him and see what you got."

Which is exactly what the skeeters did—got a fat soldier and took him out to the bushes and sucked the brother till the bones stuck out of him. And man, they came away from the feast with a buzz on. They said, "Hey, forget black blood, man; what we got here is a feast."

And every night, the soldiers would hear the drums from way off—talking drums. Sometimes from the left, it seemed, and sometimes from the right. And sometimes it seemed right on top of them. They would say to themselves, "Man, just listen to them drums. Colored people sure know how to party."

But that was no party—that was Toussaint and his men hiding out in the mountains, practicing close-order drill on the talking drums: *Tedee boom, teedee boom, right face. Tedee boom, teedee boom, left face. Tedee boom, teedee boom, forward march! Tedee boom, teedee boom, to the rear march* . . .

Big bad man they call Leclerc,
He ain't nothing but a jerk.
When the time is come to pass,
We run down and kick his ass.
When that kicking ass is through,
Find Napoléon, kick his too!

*Sound off, tedee boom boom boom. Sound off, tedee boom, teedee boom boom boom* . . . and on, and on, and on, the whole night long, getting themselves together for the great moment when the chance to fight the battle would come.

All day Leclerc's men sat around the barracks and waited—by day, it was the heat; by night, it was the mosquitoes—with nothing to do but play cards. They didn't trust the water, so they drank champagne and ate Haitian dumplings. The more of them Haitian dumplings the soldiers would eat, the sicker they would get. Some of them started dropping dead like flies, right at the dinner table.

One night, while he was listening to all them drums up in the mountains, Leclerc got an idea. His men were not only tired and bored, but also they were coming down right and left with yellow fever, dengue fever, malaria, and all the other things that the mosquitoes freely gave in exchange for a decent meal. Why not throw a big party, boost his men's morale? A catered affair, with fiddles, cognac and champagne, and candles, just like at home in Paris. That's what he did. And the little old women with bandanas on their heads, who cooked for the soldiers, they outdid themselves: black widow spider meat stewed in horse piss and garlic; beestings on a biscuit, dipped in donkey dung and stuffed in red peppers. Then the little priests brought out a big bouillabaisse—it's against voodoo law for me to tell you what was in *that!*

Now, it was a bright moonlit night, and the soldiers said, "Oh man, listen. It's a different beat up there tonight. Wow, wow, wow!"

Well, it was a different beat. Why was it different? Because some of those little children had been sent into the hills by some of those ladies smoking the pipes. And the brothers put the message on the drums: *Tedee boom, teedee boom boom boom: One more time, everybody, put nails in your broomsticks, sharpen your teeth and your toenails, grab your machetes and butcher knives, your Coca-Cola bottles and brickbats . . . Wait for the talking drums to give the signal, then MOVE!*

Leclerc heard the drums, and he knew right away something was wrong! He tried to snap to attention: "Soldiers of France, fall in!" But the soldiers of France were snoring, sound asleep. Just then, them Haitian dumplings kicked in, and he had to run outside to take care of a little business. By the time he got back to the barracks, it was too late: Toussaint, and Henri Christophe, and Jean-Jacques Dessalines were all over Leclerc and his soldiers of France like white on rice. Beat 'em so bad they barely escaped. They jumped on the boat, got the hell away from Haiti and back to France as fast as the winds would take them.

Napoléon was furious. "Fool, fool, fool! I need that sugar cane! What you doing back in France? Get back to Haiti at once!"

"No more Haiti, Nap, not for me. And if you know what's good for you, you won't go either. Anyway, Nap, if you go over there and you hear them drums, get the heck out as fast as you can."

Napoléon saw that the boy was serious. And without Haiti and its sugar cane crop, he was going to have to find a new way to fund his armies. So he sat down and he wrote a letter to Thomas Jefferson, who at that time was president of thirteen little raggedy colonies that just got through fighting Great Britain, and man they were in bad shape. And Napoléon said, "Tom boy, look—I've got this land and I want to give it to you for fifteen million dollars. Put it in a suitcase and send it."

And that's what happened. Thomas Jefferson sent him fifteen million dollars, and as a result, the U.S. came into possession of all the central portion of the country as it now stands.

Those talking drums transformed a bunch of slaves who couldn't even understand each other into a revolutionary army. It was the first time in history that slaves had freed themselves by force of arms, without help from anybody else. America and Europe never forgave Haiti for that. Not even to this day—that's one of the reasons why Haiti is still in trouble. But it was the bravery of those black men and women—who cared so much for freedom they were willing to give up their own lives—that defeated the greatest military power of its time. And out of that struggle came the United States as we know it today.

# THE WORLD OF HUNGER AND ME

*Winter 2002*

I am who they say I am: Ossie Davis, actor, writer, director, minor colored movie star celebrity, and an activist. The fires of the hell of which I dream, from which I flee, the focus of my growing agitation consists of the following words, which I found in the *New York Times* on November 8. I quote in part:

> The world population stands at 6.1 billion, double what it was in 1960. Two billion people already lack sufficient food, and water use has increased six times over the past 70 years. Fifty years from now 4.2 billion people will be living in countries where their basic needs cannot be met. "Poor people depend more directly on natural resources such as available land, wood and water, and yet they suffer most from environmental degradation," said Thoraya Obaid, executive director of the United Nations Population Fund in its annual report. The increasing impact on the environment resulted not only from growing population, but also from "rising affluence and unsustainable consumption patterns."
>
> "The world's wealth is some $30 trillion, but half the world lives on $2 a day or less. The message here is clear,"

she added. "While some of us practice wasteful consumption, others cannot consume enough to survive."*

If this report is true, it would seem to me that the world as I know it is being divided more and more between the haves and the have-nots. Which seems to indicate that sooner rather than later I, my children, and my grandchildren will have to decide: Which side are we on? Are we on the side of the haves—including my own native land, America, where 6 percent of the world's population consumes 35 percent of its resources without taking a second thought? Or do we, simply because we are black—and racism being racism—do we belong to the have-nots, the great majority of whom earn $2 a day or less?

Which side am I on? Or is it really necessary—since I am an actor, a writer, a director, a colored movie star celebrity, talent for sale, image for hire, celebrity for rent to the highest bidder, doing piece work on the Hollywood plantation—is it really necessary for me to make a choice? Maybe I can remain suspended, far above it all. Secure in the knowledge that I am an American—that I have rights and privileges protected by the Constitution and by the greatest pile of money and military might in human history? That no matter what is happening to the rest of the world down among the have-nots, the white folks like me, and the rich folks like me; I am doing all right. Which side of the great and growing divide between those who got it and those who ain't am I on?

---

*Copyright © 2002 by The New York Times Co. Reprinted with permission.

I know how Harriet Tubman would have answered. When she was a free person up north, and the rest of us were still stuck in bondage and in slave pens down south, she could have sided with the haves and left us slaves to the mercy of our masters. She could have stayed up north and made a life for herself, but no. She sneaked back into Maryland, time and time again, freed her people a few slaves at a time, and led them to freedom at the risk of her own life. I know which side she was on.

I know how old John Brown would have answered in his day. The man who could have become a prosperous farmer and remained at home in New England like thousands of others did. Or he could have been a slaveholder himself, growing rich off the unpaid labor of my ancestor. But instead, he formed his own little brigade and went down to Harpers Ferry to try and free the slaves. It cost him his life, but never once did he look back. I know which side he was on.

And what about Frederick Douglass? He escaped from slavery in Maryland and went north, where he, too, could have chosen to stay put and make a name and a life for himself and his family. But no, not Frederick Douglass. He was a newspaper man, an orator, and an agitator. He wouldn't let the country rest as he boldly put himself in harm's way, raging up and down demanding freedom for his enslaved brothers and sisters, until he finally got it. I know which side he was on.

And W.E.B. Du Bois, who helped to found the NAACP, created a magazine, which he called *The Crisis,* and used it—sometimes like a scalpel and sometimes like a sledgehammer—in a frontal assault against lynching, Jim Crow, and institutional segregation until the walls came tumbling down in the

Supreme Court's *Brown v. Board of Education* decision of 1954. He could have remained a quiet, learned professor at Atlanta University, could have been preferred among the rich and powerful industrialists from the north, like Booker T. Washington. But not W.E.B.

And what about A. Philip Randolph, who went to jail for his writings on behalf of the poor and the dispossessed, then formed a union to lead them in their fight to escape from poverty; and Mary McLeod Bethune, who took her people's cause all the way to the White House, where, instead of being quiet and polite, she agitated for the rights of African-Americans; and Marian Anderson, who stood out in the cold Easter morning on the steps of the Lincoln Memorial after being turned down because of her color by the Daughters of the American Revolution, and sang the story of her have-not brothers and sisters, about the freedom we still didn't have; and Paul Robeson, who never sang a word that was not also a weapon in his fight for all the dispossessed peoples of the Earth—even when they took his passport, he still found a way to sing all the way across the ocean by telephone.

And most certainly Martin Luther King, Jr., who recognized the poor, the despised, the rejected, and the forgotten as his brothers, and was on his way to Washington as champion of their cause, when brutal assassins tracked him into Memphis, and there shot him down. And Malcolm X too. And Fannie Lou Hamer. They saw the world being divided between the haves and the have-nots and stood on the corners screaming till they died. There is no question which side they were on.

But now the same question, which faced these mighty warriors for Justice, Equality, and Freedom, faces me. Am I required, as they were, in defense of what I believe, to put my life on the line? September 11, 2001, leaves me no hiding place. Civilization itself hangs in the balance: it cannot exist in a world half rich and half starving.

I leave you with the question still unanswered, hanging above my mirror, my conscience, and my mind. In a world where half the people live on $2 a day, or less, which side am I on? Which side are you on?

# WHAT I FOUND ON THIS CAMPUS

～

*Howard University, Annenberg Lecture Series*
*2003*

R.D.: *When the invitation came for Ossie to participate in the Annenberg Lecture Series at Howard University, several days passed before he shared the information with me. I understood. We'd been invited together and separately through the years—he to speak at graduations, special celebrations, and programs. Two of my most memorable times were also at Howard: first, conducting a theatre workshop for actors, and then writing and directing* Zora Is My Name, *a theatre piece based on works by Zora Neale Hurston that was later picked up by PBS for its* American Playhouse *television series. Together, we filmed several specials for Howard's own television station, WHMM-TV (now WHUT). We also filmed some of the best segments of* With Ossie & Ruby, *the public television series we were privileged to produce for three years. We dreamed of a permanent television and film company located at Howard.*

*There was no doubt in either of our minds, despite Ossie's occasional reference to his not having graduated, that he was a natural-born teacher.*

Thank you, Dean Dates, and thank you, students. It's quite a delight to be here and hear all of those words rolled over me while I'm still alive. I have taken this assignment quite seriously. Usually, I depend merely on my memory and a quick-witted dance off the top of my head to give the impression that I know a great deal about what I'm talking about, but I respected you too much for that. My thoughts, I have decided to commit to the printed page, and I'm going to share some of them with you right now. Bear with me, if you please.

*Hello, my name is Ossie Davis* . . .

The subject that brings us together is education, but I am no expert and, I suspect, neither are you. My object is to add the thing or two I know to the thing or two you know, so perhaps we can both learn from my experience. I owe a debt of more than gratitude to this university, a debt I want you to help me pay. I came to this campus in 1935 to get something very important. I didn't exactly know what it was that I was after when I came, but those who did called it an education; and although I never got a degree—I never graduated in a cap and gown, never got a diploma or certificate—I got what I came for. And when I did, I left.

There is no way for me to calculate the value of what I got when I was here, especially in terms of money—I never paid tuition. I was on a National Youth Administration scholarship, a program that gave scholarships to pay tuition for students all over the country who qualified by the work they did in high school, but had no money. And this was in the middle of the Depression. So I showed up at the college gate with a whole host of other people who didn't have any money. And lo and behold, they let me in.

Howard gave to me, fully and freely when I needed it, my

liberation and my identification—things I needed to have to begin my life as a black man. What I'd like to do now is to pass a little of what I learned on to you in the form of this lecture, to share with you the story of my life those many years ago on this campus. I wanted to share my other self, not the one I am now, older, wiser, and full of obligations, honors, and arthritis; but the lucky little black boy from Waycross, Georgia, who lived in 1935, who was even then—although he hadn't the slightest idea—a vital part of Negro history and of the black experience, the predominant part of which was education.

My education was much like that of tens of thousands of other black boys and girls in the South, reading, writing, arithmetic, geography, spelling, and plenty of annual doses of Negro History Week. The poetry of Phillis Wheatley and of Paul Laurence Dunbar, the stirring orations of Frederick Douglass, the burning heroic deeds of Harriet Tubman, Toussaint-Louverture, Nat Turner, and Booker T. Washington.

There was, of course, another curriculum to which I was constantly exposed that the black community didn't talk so much about: lynchings, the Ku Klux Klan, rape, and murder. The grown-ups—preachers, teachers, Mama, and Daddy—didn't have an easy vocabulary on these dark and violent subjects. Nobody could say exactly why the white folks hated us so much or when it would all be over. We only knew that from time to time the niggerization of black folks reached out and touched us all. This is how it reached out one day and touched me.

One day, when I was no more than six or seven, on my way home from school, two policemen called out to me from their car, "Come here, boy! Come over here." They told me to get into the car and drove me down to the precinct. There was no threat or intimidation in them and I was not afraid, neither was I upset. They laughed at me, but the laughter didn't seem mean or vindictive. It indicated the fun we all were having. They kept me there for about an hour. No attempt was made to call my mama, who might very well have been worried that I had not come home from school.

Later, in their joshing around, laughing at me and me laughing at myself, one of them reached for a bottle of cane syrup and poured the contents over my head. This time they laughed even louder, as if it was the funniest thing in the world, and I laughed too. Then the joke was over. The ritual was complete. They gave me several chunks of peanut brittle, which I ate with great relish, and then they let me go. I was never made to feel afraid. My feelings weren't hurt. It seemed perfectly all right.

And yet, something very wrong had been done to me, something which to this day I never forgot. I never talked about it to anybody, even my friends. It always seemed a secret, too deep, too intimate for me to discuss even with myself. But what happened to me in the police precinct was the building block of all my education, the heart of which I brought with me to Howard University—central, subconscious, leaving scars, the marks of niggerization I carry with me always.

Now, nobody came out and said it directly to me, but in a very important way, the whole adventure of black education was an attempt—by white folks and black—to help relieve me of this trauma, this non–self-healing damage that lay like a stone at the bottom of my identity. The prospect of recovery began for me right here on this campus, where I was met and taken under wing by mentors who knew my condition better than they knew my name, three extraordinary men: Mordecai Johnson, Sterling Brown, and Alain LeRoy Locke.

Now, when I came on the campus in 1935, I was welcomed with open arms and took what I thought was full advantage of the new atmosphere to which I was finally exposed. I didn't know exactly what I wanted to be, but I knew that when I found it, I would know what it was. So there I was on campus—in front of me a smorgasbord of books and peoples and new ways of life, and I was determined to experience it all. The first year my major was English. The second year my major was philosophy. The third year my major was psychology. As you see, I majored all over the place. I was greedy: I took what pleased me, and I consumed it in copious quantities. There were books by black people, stories about black people, and then of course there were books from the general canon, Shakespeare, English poetry, all of these things to which I was suddenly exposed.

One of my first instructors was Sterling Brown, a poet on the campus. I liked him right away because somehow he reminded me of my father. Studying with Sterling Brown introduced me to material that was already crammed into my life, the stories I had heard from my mother and my father, the music that I experienced on the working gangs down south and in the cotton field, all of that humor and the jokes, the ghost stories that I knew . . . Sterling told me this was not only material black folks wasted time with; this was literature. And that opened a door in my head that has yet to be closed. It expanded my consciousness and made me a more important person, even to myself.

Sterling would instruct his class by indirection, by jokes, by innuendos, by discussing with us things that were happening on the world stage that affected black people in terms of humor, putting into our consciousness information we desperately needed if we were to understand what the world was all about.

He was a master storyteller, Sterling; he was full of stories and they were always funny stories. And I came from a family where my father was a master storyteller, my mother was a master storyteller. I had a head full of stories just like Sterling's. So I said wow, wow, that's for me—whatever Sterling was into, that's what I wanted to be into, too.

I did my first writing in Sterling Brown's class. I wrote some poetry and slipped it under his door. He invited me to his office and we sat down and talked, not so much about my poetry, I mean Sterling was not so great an actor as to make believe that what I had written was worthy of serious consideration, but he got a glimpse from what I wrote of the kind of person I was. And he responded to me not only as a professor, but as a friend and as a mentor. I became one of those students invited to go to his home on various occasions and go down into the basement and listen to his collection of blues and jazz, and talk about drinking Wild Turkey. I got to love him and I got to be a devotee of his and we remained friends until he died. So it was Sterling Brown who lit the first fire of artistic consciousness in my mind. But before I got to Sterling, in a way, I got to a man who didn't teach classes, but he was the president of the university, Mordecai Johnson.

Think Moses, a little lawgiver, coming down from Sinai with the tablets of the law. Mordecai looked and acted as if he truly were the voice of God, visiting the campus for a genial inspection of what was going on in God's heaven. And as he walked across the campus, tipping his hat and smiling to the young ladies, we boys knew that that was the way we were supposed to behave toward young ladies, too. We knew that Mordecai was setting us all an example; and there was something about him that almost commanded that we, if we wanted to consider ourselves true men, would live up to his standard of deportment, of his respect for women, of his respect for learning, of the way he walked and stood and carried himself.

His kind of leadership seemed demanded by the tenor of the times, which were uncertain and foreboding: with the Depression, and the war clouds gathering over Europe, Asia, and Africa, people sought for something to have unquestionable faith in—something only strong, unhesitant leadership could provide. There was Franklin Delano Roosevelt in America; Adolf Hitler in Germany; Haile Selassie in Africa; the Emperor Hirohito in Japan; Stalin in Russia; and for us students here on the campus, there was Mordecai Johnson, reared against the eastern sky.

He was the first black president of Howard University. And that was an item of importance. When slavery ended, whites from the North and the South came down south to help us.

Colleges were instituted. This institution itself came into being, to feed the hungry need of blacks for an education as the one way out. And the white teachers and preachers and educational authorities had the advantage of the protection provided by the federal government. But after the federal troops went away, and Jim Crow laws were put on the books in the South, little by little these white teachers—whose job it was to help us create black teachers and black professors and black folks who would take the responsibility of leadership—began to be consistent with the mores and the anti-black sentiments of the white South.

And little by little it became apparent to us that what we needed was to take our affairs out of the hands of the whites who had come to help us—or who had profited by a position—and to institute instead teachers, preachers, school presidents from our own group, even on this particular campus. Men like Carter G. Woodson, who, desirous of teaching students like you black history, was denied that opportunity by the Board of Trustees, and he resigned. Can you imagine on a black campus not being able to teach children black history? Because the Board of Trustees thought that blacks didn't have enough history to worry about—and what history they had was so negative that they shouldn't be learning that at all. What kind of leadership would that provide to the young black students?

Well, finally in 1926 things came to a head and they brought in Mordecai Johnson, the first black president of Howard University. But Mordecai didn't come merely to serve as the first president of black folks. He knew that a part of his responsibility was to teach the qualities of leadership to black students in a way that the whites could not teach it, to give them an image of their capacity to solve their problems and to be responsible for themselves. So when Mordecai Johnson walked up and down the campus, he was not just being the head of Howard University. He was setting an example to the students of black independent thought, of black courage, of our own capacity to provide and teach leadership to our own students.

So I was a part of what Mordecai Johnson had come on the campus ten years before to prove—that black instructors and black presidents and black figures of authority could effect a change among blacks in the black community. Nobody sat me down and told me all that, but I hope I behaved properly when I was on the campus with the other students.

Now a third mentor was Alain LeRoy Locke. He was not a buddy, not a fellow storyteller like Sterling, nor a strong father figure like Mordecai. He was a scholar, a Rhodes scholar, and he exemplified the life of a scholar. He specialized in aesthetics, and he was especially convinced that black people had aesthetic gifts that put them on the level with whites and sometimes above. He had been educated at German universities and he saw how the Europeans respected African art and African culture, not like in America.

Dr. Locke was determined not only to teach a new aesthetic, not only to teach the white folks about the glories of blackness, but to teach the black folks, too. He understood that when we came from slavery we were crippled, we felt ourselves inferior, that we were hurt, that the syrup on the little boy's head had changed his life forever. But he felt that if he could get to the people the truth about themselves and about the culture they could produce, it would change the people and they would become new Negroes.

So he wrote the book *The New Negro;* and the new Negro was the Negro like Mordecai Johnson and like Sterling Brown—those who demanded the right to speak as leaders to their own people in their own names and in their own personae, to show that black was historic and powerful and beautiful. And so a part of what Locke did was to spread the gospel of black sufficiency in the arts everywhere he went. He was one of the people who went around discovering talent. He discovered Zora Neale Hurston. He went all the way to Paris to find a young poet working in the kitchen named Langston Hughes. And when he found them, he found ways to help them survive because he knew that they were soldiers in the battle to prove the equality of our people.

I don't know what it was that he saw in me, but once after I passed a test with flying colors, he invited me to his office, sat me down, and asked me what I wanted to do with myself. And by that time I was sufficiently knowledgeable to tell him that I wanted to be a writer and that I wanted to write plays. He was a little astounded when he heard that, because in listening to my accent he knew right away that I had come from Big Foot country and therefore might not really know what writing plays was about.

So he pushed me on the point. He said, "Have you ever been to a theatre?"

And I said, "Yes sir, a theatre down in Waycross. Every Saturday night I go to see the cowboy pictures."

He said, "I don't mean cowboys, I don't mean pictures. I mean live people up on the stage."

I said, "Well, we put on some Shakespeare in the high school."

He said, "Have you seen people onstage who are acting out a drama, telling a story?" And I said no.

Now, at the time on this campus were the Howard Players, one of the first groups of American artists to be sent overseas by the State Department, going overseas to Sweden to do plays. I'm on the campus, getting ready to be a playwright; I didn't even know the existence of the Howard Players.

Dr. Locke sort of shook his head and said, "Ossie, I'll tell you what. I'll make a suggestion to you. When you finish here, I want you to go to Harlem. There's a little theatre group, they're called the Rose McClendon Players. I want you to ask them to let you join, and if they do, you join, you do everything you possibly can—act, sing, dance, paint scenery, build sets, sell lemonade, whatever. And that way you'll find out what the theatre is and learn whether you can write for it or not."

Well, all of a sudden something happened in my mind. I was so convinced that that specifically was what I had come to college to find, I decided then and there that I didn't need any further exposure to all the other intellectual goodies offered to me on the campus. I didn't bother to stay and graduate. I didn't. I went to Harlem. I found that little group recommended by Dr. Alain LeRoy Locke. I joined it. I was inducted at that time and place into the theatre, where I have been ever since.

So you see, although I didn't graduate from Howard University, it was Dr. Alain LeRoy Locke who specifically gave me placement in the theatre for which I was being prepared. So it was still, in my mind, a Howard activity. I chose Easter Sunday, 1939, to leave. However, an incident happened that made me delay my departure.

I think students had invited Marian Anderson to sing in a church nearby, but the church burned down so there was no place for Marian Anderson to sing. They went instead down to Constitution Hall, owned by the Daughters of the American Revolution, and asked for permission for Marian Anderson to sing. And of course, you know the story. The Daughters said no, you can't do that. Well, at that, Eleanor Roosevelt, who was a member of the Daughters, resigned, and got Harold Ickes—who dealt with parks—to let them hold the concert at the Lincoln Memorial on Easter.

So it was that on the Sunday I had chosen to leave town, Marian Anderson was consigned to sing at the Lincoln Memorial. It was a cold day, but I stayed, delayed my departure to be at the concert, along with 75,000 other people. And as I listened, I became aware of a conversion, of a feeling in me of empowerment that I never knew before. Something of my incapacities dropped off, and something of my lack of self-assertion disappeared. Something appeared inside me like a strong fist in me and pulled me up to my feet.

She was an artist. She was what Locke was talking about. She was the power that he had promised could be used in the struggle. And I wanted to be one of that number.

There's a phrase in W.E.B. Du Bois's Credo that can express better than I can the feeling that moment when Marian Anderson lifted me. That phrase tells what happened to me on this campus—what Locke was trying to do and what Mordecai was trying to do and what Sterling was trying to do: "I believe in the training of children," Du Bois says, "black even as white; the leading out of little souls into the green pastures and beside the still waters, not for pelf or peace, but for Life lit by some large vision of beauty and goodness and truth."

What I found on this campus was that vision, a glimpse of what it could be and a glimpse of my relationship to it. And it claimed me, it defined me, it illuminated me, it set me on a course from which I have not deviated.

So all that I have done, all that I have experienced, all that I have created, all that I have been connected to in its best phase is an example of my response to the light that's shone on me, that life lit by some large vision of beauty and goodness and truth which Mordecai and Sterling and Alain Locke were waiting to hand me when I arrived on campus in 1935.

And as it happened to me, so should and must it happen to you. I would be derelict in my duty if I did not try to pass on to the young generation what was passed on to me.

I just got in the mail today a request from a congressman, and he is going to have a very important conference dealing with the state of the African-American male. He's asked me to be one of the speakers. Let me read you just one paragraph of that letter: "What is happening with African-American males? The state of the African-American male, a yearlong national dialogue. Why are 32 percent of African-American males unemployed? Why are 40 percent of African-American males in the criminal justice system either on probation or parole or in prison? Why are so many African-American boys on the low end of the literacy scale and dropping out of school? Why do so many black men die earlier of diseases that are treatable?"

As I read that I'm swept back to my own history, to a little boy in the basement of a police precinct with syrup being poured on his head to teach him a lesson about who he was and who he wasn't, and the process of niggerization that went on at that time. And I ask myself, is the process still working? Has there not been sufficient change to liberate the black man? Is there something in our history, in our culture and our psyches that still must be faced? Is there something that I found on this campus that could apply itself to the solution of these problems? These problems which define the world in which you and I are living now will not remain static—they will increase in severity, or they will go away.

A lot of the hope for a positive future depends upon those of us who still have, or have access to, some concept of life lit by some large vision of truth and goodness and beauty. Is there a way that we from this campus, with the powers that we have, can reach over the prison walls and down into the cells and bring life lit by some large vision? What is the responsibility now of this university? What would old Mordecai say if he were invited to speak? What would Sterling say? What would Alain LeRoy Locke say?

And so I come to you, glad to share the story of an important part of my life, how I was affected by the time I spent on this campus and who I met when I got here. But I do not look back with sentimental attachment to the past. I look forward. I come not to celebrate the past, but to examine it, to see if somewhere in it there's still some clue that will help us reach out to the African-American male and extend to him some vision of life lit by some large purpose, some large interconnectedness, to welcome him back to the family.

And now, having said all that, I'd like for you to respond. I'd like perhaps that you might ask some questions to which I could give answer. I'll try to be as truthful as possible.

Yes . . . ?

# CONVOCATION SPEECH

~

*Howard University Charter Day 2004*
*March 5, 2004*

M r. President, Board of Trustees, faculty, students, and friends:

We note with extreme delight that the turning of the season, the passing of the years, have finally brought that singular anniversary that stands in our regard like a second emancipation, which we as a people should be more than glad to remember. For it was the seventeenth of May, in the year of our Lord 1954, that grandeur raised its voice and spoke the truth.

The Supreme Court, which had not always been the black man's friend and neighbor, was all of a sudden the conscience of the nation, raising its voice, and in speaking for the nation spoke for us all.

*Brown v. Board of Education.* The words are made of wood, but still they sing of an angelic high point in American jurisprudence. *Brown v. Board of Education:* awkward, stiff, and legalistic, hardly the appropriate title for a poem; but it should be. This is a thing the soul should celebrate—time has worked its magic-rendering judgment, in the parlance of the people.

Whoever touched the case became a hero; wherever it walked, the place was holy ground. How proud we are, we here at Howard University, to be standing a single stone's throw away from where history first threw the gauntlet down. Where inspiration and determination raised their first faint flag. Where Howard Law was born to answer prayer.

Howard Law—note well the name. Fifty years ago it was, the courts spoke and out of their unanimous mouths came *Brown v. Board of Education:* We hold that in the field of public education, separate is inherently unequal and has no place. That was Howard Law. How long, America, did it take you to see the simple fact and say it clear? Oh, let us mark the day and hold it hallowed!

Now, it was natural that the showdown between black folks and the American Constitution had to come, and when it came the battlefield would be education. It's always been about education—even more than about wealth, or servitude and status, and family, creed, and color; knowledge has always been power. We knew that then, we know that now. And that is why this celebration, at this time and in this place, is so important. Knowledge is power and as such holds every key to every chain and shackle; it always did, it always will.

We knew, even then—even when we were slaves—that if we could find what the master kept hidden in the books beside his bed, we could get a taste of the freedom he enjoyed, and we wouldn't be slaves no more. No matter what you called it—they knew it, we knew it. It was as simple as that. And so, what the Civil War had started with guns and cannons and bayonets, we planned to finish with books. Slavery had left its stigma in us and on us, but give us a book and we would wash it clean.

So it was when four million of us left the plantation to join the quarter million already free, freedom to us meant getting an education. And there were many, white and black, who helped us along our journey. Schools, academies, institutes, and here and there a college where possible, and even a few who set themselves up as universities: Fisk, Atlanta, Hampton, and of course, Howard. Howard University.

Howard: midwife, wet nurse, mother. Was ever another American university called upon to involve itself more deeply in the birthing of a people? To make itself more umbilical, urging us on from cotton patch to culture? Was Harvard? Was Princeton? Was Yale? Howard University, created to do a great service to the country. A service that led by hook—and sometimes by crook—straight to the doorway of the American Constitution and, through the door, to *Brown v. Board of Education*. That is the story of Howard Law, and this is where it began. The vigil keepers and how they kept the watch. This is the story, but it still has a villain. Let us reconsider.

For a moment, after the Civil War, it seemed that black citizenship had come into its own. The Thirteenth Amendment ending slavery, the Fourteenth Amendment making all citizens equal, and the Fifteenth Amendment giving us the right to vote had been added to the basic tally of the law of the land.

But then, strange things began to happen. Men—good, solid Americans who thought they wished us well—ran head-on into the American dilemma hidden in their bosom. They could accept the black man's right to be free, but when we asserted our equal right to be equal under the Fourteenth Amendment, they froze, caught in the trammels of greed and jealous contradictions. Little by little, the laws became subverted. The liberties we had won were compromised and, one by one, began to be taken away. That's when we learned this puzzling thing about liberty: the less you have to begin with, the more chance you have of losing what remains. You fight like hell to protect the right to fight.

We watched with deep dismay as Jim Crow, segregation, and discrimination, and lynching, and racism little by little began eating away at all our rights and privileges. Yes, we were citizens right enough, but citizens second class—the status of the powerless and the oppressed.

We begged, we petitioned, we sued, hoping against hope to find refuge in the Constitution, that the Fourteenth Amendment—created for that purpose—would come to our aid and rescue. But fortune set its stony face against us. The Supreme Court, when it spoke, spoke with forked tongue, slamming the door in our faces. They called it *Plessy v. Ferguson.* They said that regarding our basic rights, the separated-segregated Jim Crow world to which we had been consigned was plenty good enough. In 1896, "separate but equal" became the law of the land. We knew it was a crime, we knew it was a lie, a world split down the middle, but it was all we had. So, we set out to make this wickedness work to our advantage. Eternal vigilance was the heavy price we paid. And Howard Law set out to become the people's tongue and the people's eyes.

And what a cast of characters this hallowed institution provided.

Let's start off with that giant of a man, Howard University president Mordecai Johnson, the first African-American to hold that office. He looked upon the Howard Law School—which had been there since the very beginning—and found it wanting. He made it a three-year day school and promoted Charles Hamilton Houston and put him in charge. Charles brought another brilliant legal mind, William Hastie. The two men were cousins, and they had a protégé whom they both loved, Thurgood Marshall. Then there was Oliver Hill, James Nabrit, and others. And Howard Law was the place they all intersected and plotted and argued and strategized, and from which they scurried off to battle.

They took separate-but-equal as a racist insult, an outrage which lived beyond the law and common sense. They swore they would attack it on its own presumptions, and they did. According to *Plessy v. Ferguson,* black folks could be legally excluded from every amenity the states offered white folks— schools, colleges, universities, buses, books, and libraries—as long as these amenities were also offered to blacks in equal measure. That's what it said; but one look at what was really happening showed that's not what it meant. In almost every case, what blacks received was, in almost every way, less and inferior to what whites got.

Black leadership saw the contradiction and went on the attack. If the South really wanted two school systems instead of one, then they could be forced to pay for two school systems instead of one. Howard Law set out to make them live up to their constitutional obligations. And fifty years ago, the highest court went even further than that—and gave America a chance to save its soul—in a decision which became the sparkplug of a revolution that changed this country forever.

You may say, under those circumstances, who needs now

Howard University? It's all done, it's all taken care of. But no-body understands America, its good points and its bad, better than black folks. Attention must always be paid. No, now is not the time to take Howard from us, now is not the time to take away our guardian, now is not the time to take away the vigil keepers. Strange things are happening in the land. New laws are being proposed, laws which attack the very basic fundamentals of our freedom. Somebody must keep watch, somebody must stand up, somebody must protest. Who—from the experience in the past—would be more qualified than Howard Law to do just that?

The basic promise of *Brown* has yet to be advanced. Now as then, Howard Law is the people's watch, continuing—great vigil-keepers all—with deep and sleepless eyes, our shield and buckler against all inquisitions, all "patriotic acts" that say one thing but truly mean another. It is now we need the watchers, now we need the couriers, now we need those who understand fully that the price of freedom is always eternal vigilance. Howard University has more experience of being black and making the most of it than any other institution in the country that I know.

Howard University, Howard Law:

> Reared against the eastern sky,
> Proudly there on hilltop high.
> Howard Law—still firm and true
> Keeping watch for me and you.

Thank you.

# A DISCUSSION WITH YOUNG
# ACTIVISTS AND ARTISTS

~

*Detroit, June 2003*

When I came along, the focus of much of our attention was to prove to ourselves and to the world that we could do whatever anyone else could do, as well if not better. We knew that the world judged us by our behavior. When I was involved in the theatre, I knew that how we spoke and the way we dressed and behaved had to be different from the stereotypes with which we were surrounded, stereotypes that implied that we were backward and stupid, and that we couldn't rise to any occasion that required thought and skill.

We were bound by our circumstances. Our teachers expected us to behave up to a certain standard. Our fellow craftsman was Paul Robeson, and we wanted to do it like Paul, whose art came from the people and led back to the people. We were tremendously influenced by that as a concept.

We could not conceive or entertain the idea of Art for Art's sake. When Marian Anderson sang a song, we knew that there was struggle and pain and death and resurrection involved in her singing. And as we listened to her, we knew that she was speaking out of the depths of her experiences, which belonged to us as they did to her. She was singing to and for her people.

It was impossible to think of Marian Anderson singing for the sake of singing. We knew that.

The Harlem Renaissance was based upon that premise. We wanted to show the American people that we had a command of the arts that qualified us as human beings.

This was the journey we were on. It wasn't a question of being stars or celebrities. It was a question of being onstage and saying something positive about our people that we wanted the world to hear. So my motivation was to use the arts as a part of our struggle, and it has remained that for me ever since.

I know that there has been a change in our opportunities and possibilities. Young people who come along now have no responsibility to anyone but themselves. I understand that; but that was not a possibility when I came along. A lot of what I was involved in helped change the situation so that those who only want to express themselves now have the chance to do so.

But in 1947, a young man like Jackie Robinson had to swallow his tongue because everything he said, every step he took, every time he swung his bat, every base he stole, was a message to the world. The thought that Jackie was out there only to get the millions now available was inconceivable. It was the same with Joe Louis. Every time he stepped into the ring, every blow he landed was a blow for freedom. He was our spokesman, saying to the world, "This is who we are."

Whether we wanted to or not, we knew that the journey of our people was in our hands, positively or negatively. We were aware of that; and it influenced our conduct, onstage and off. And to some degree, that still applies.

# ESSAYS

*In theater at its best we experience, through our imagination, the* feel *of what is true. And having felt it, we know it; and having known it, we possess it—and are possessed by it—forever.*

*Once I feel the truth, the internal* is-ness of, *say, a Negro, a Jew, a Gentile, a Catholic, a Communist, a homosexual, or a Nazi, I can no longer pretend that he is a stranger, or a foreigner, or an outcast. What is more, I will be so pleasured in my new knowledge that I would not want to so pretend. I will myself have become, at one and the same time, all of these things.*

*There is at this very moment at the heart of our very affluent society a silent sickness. Thirty to forty million of our people live in poverty. But they do not live in poverty* for me! *They scream, but I cannot hear them; they hunger, but I feel no pang for them; they die, but they die beyond my comprehension. They are strangers and foreigners and outsiders, and will so remain until some poet, some painter, some actor makes me* feel *their presence. When, through my imagination, I am led to* feel *their silent desperation, then only will I know them and recognize them as a part of myself.*

—IN THE *NEW YORK TIMES*, AUGUST 23, 1964

# PURLIE TOLD ME

Freedomways, *Spring 1962*

Nothing I had learned from the Baptist Bible, from Howard University, from my long association with causes, black and white, or from my fifteen years on Broadway, prepared me in any degree for what I was to learn from Purlie Victorious—as actor, as author, as Negro, and as what I hope someday soon to be—a man!

Had not Purlie come along when he did, and proceeded to shake the living daylight out of me, I would by now have had it made: I would have sidestepped completely the Negro Question (which is, to the best of my knowledge, "When the hell are we gonna be free?!"); I would have safely escaped into the Negro middle class, burying my head somewhere between the Cadillac and the mink; and I would probably have become, by express permission and endorsement of the Great White Father, an honorary white man myself. But Purlie came, Purlie saw, Purlie laughed!

In pursuit of Purlie I found more than I had bargained for: the act of writing became my long moment of truth; and it took me five years to adjust my eyesight, to be able to look squarely at the world, and at myself, through Negro-colored glasses. And to decide, on the basis of what I found: it is not enough to be only a Negro in this world . . . one must, and more importantly, also be a man.

For Purlie Victorious is, in essence, the adventures of Negro manhood in search of itself in a world for white folks only. A world that emasculated me, as it does all Negro men, before I left my mother's breast; and which had taught me to gleefully accept that emasculation as the highest honor America could bestow upon a black man. And in more ways than I thought possible, I had accepted it!

Purlie, in order to get himself put down on paper at all, had to force me to examine myself; to dig deeper and deeper into my own soul, conscious and subconscious, to peel off and rip away layer after layer of sham, hypocrisy, evasion, lies—to rip up by the root the many walls I had erected around the pretense that I was indeed a man—when I knew all along— but had never been before forced to admit even to myself— that in the context of American Society today, *the term Negro and the term Man must mutually exclude each other!*

Purlie showed me that, whatever I was, I was not a man . . . not yet! That I would never become a man by sacrificing everything I was, merely to become an American. That I would never ease my way into the bosom of American acceptance by pretending, like Jacob, that I was Esau; by pretending that freedom and equality could be practiced between whites and blacks purely on a personal basis; that Negroes could be integrated into American society one at a time; that the doors of opportunity would open wider and wider each day, not only for me, but also for my brothers, as soon as we learned to talk middle-class talk, dress middle-class dress, behave middle-class behavior, and, literally, to "wash ourselves whiter than snow." And above all never to become too clamorously assertive of our rights as Americans, lest it upset those brave and leading souls of other races who know so much better how to conduct our struggles than we do!

Purlie told me I would never find my manhood by asking the white man to define it for me. That I would never become a man until I stopped measuring my black self by white standards—standards set deeply in my own mind by a racist society, which could almost define itself by its hatred and its fear of me! *And therefore felt impelled to teach me hatred and fear of myself!*

Purlie told me my *manhood* was hidden within my *Negroness,* and that I could never find the one without fully and passionately embracing the other. That only by turning again homeward, whatever the cost, to my own blackness, to my own people, and to our common experience as Negroes, could I come at last to my manhood—to my *Self!*

Purlie is black laughter, and like all laughter, when it is humane, it is liberative. Or intends to be. Based on the simple assumption that segregation is ridiculous, because it makes perfectly wonderful people, black and white, do ridiculous things, Purlie would hold all those "ridiculous things" up to universal scorn, while at the same time maintaining a loving respect for the people, white and black, caught up in this ridiculous nonsense. And when I see people, white and black, sit down side by side and laugh like hell at those ridiculous customs which still serve to keep us artificially separated, then I feel Purlie has done his job. For if men may really laugh together at something disturbing to them both it means that—

for the moment—they have overleapt their separateness; and are—for the moment—free to behold the universe, with sorrow or with joy—from the same point of view. Laughter, if it is wise, can lead to many things, even among strangers—not the least of which is that mutual respect for people on which all other relations, including the struggle for freedom in this country, must ultimately depend.

In the objective sense, the public response to Purlie, pro and con, black and white, has been no less educational. The Critics, with one exception, were highly praiseful. (Some for the wrong reasons.) And since these gentlemen usually hold in their hands the decision whether a play will live or die, their enthusiastic reception of Purlie was, in realistic terms indeed, the kiss of life. I was disappointed that they did not comment on Purlie—good, bad, or indifferent—as *literature;* and more deeply disappointed that most of the white playwrights I had known, with two exceptions—men who were friends and mentors of mine, and whose opinion I still value highly—were silent, and still are. But it is quite possible, and I say this without rancor, that their very talents, and their concepts of what a Negro is, left them unprepared to understand Purlie at all!

The theatre-going public, when it has taken the time to come and see, has usually been both surprised and delighted that comedy—satire in particular—could be such an effective weapon against race prejudice; that a stereotype about Negro life, which would be offensive in the hands of a white writer, might become, in the hands of a Negro writer, a totally unexpected revelation of the true substance of Negro wit and humor.

But Purlie, in spite of excellent reviews and a tremendous word-of-mouth enthusiasm generating from those who have seen it, has never been a big "hit" with the "carriage trade," the "expense account crowd"; and though we had some early support from theatre parties, it was not enough to really see us through. As a matter of fact, had Purlie been forced to rely on the normal avenue of Broadway patronage we would long ago have sunk and disappeared from sight. But something happened with Purlie that was different. And that difference, small as it was in the beginning, has steadily grown, until finally it made all the difference in the world.

Sylvester Leaks and John H. Clarke met Purlie firsthand on opening night, and decided he belonged to the Negro people. That decision made the difference. They went to churches, to lodges, to social clubs, labor unions. They took Purlie directly to the Negro community, and the Negro community got the message. It was, and is, the attendance of *my own people* at the box office that made the difference: it kept Purlie alive. Did this mean that a Negro work, with Negro content, could depend on the Negro community for support, and survive? I believe it did.

Not that Purlie is a Negro play only. It is, I hope, much more than that. As Purlie, himself, told me: "Look at the Negro from outside and all you see is oppression. But look at the Negro from the inside, and all you see is resistance to that oppression." Now, oppression, and the resistance to oppression, are universal themes. If Purlie speaks at all, he speaks to everybody—black and white: and the white audience still finds its merry way to the Longacre Theatre. But it is no longer always in the majority. Normally a black performer on Broadway will have his wages paid in white money. But for Purlie the situation is reversed. For the first time since I started working in the theatre, *my boss is the Negro people!*

And I choose to believe that this fact has implications for the Negro artist, musician, performer—in his struggle to express himself and survive at the same time—that are revolutionary. For if we can, in fact, create for our own people, work for our own people, belong to our own people, we will no longer be forced into artistic prostitution and self-betrayal in the mad scramble, imposed upon us far too long, to belong to some other people. We can indeed, as long as we truly deserve the support of our own, embrace our blackness, and find the stuff of our manhood.

The Negro people, if given a chance, will cherish, defend, and protect its own; Purlie is proof of that. If we turn to them ever so little, they will turn to us in full. It is time for us who call ourselves artists, scholars, and thinkers to rejoin the people from which we came. We shall then, and only then, be free to tell the truth about our people, and that truth shall make us free!

Only then can we begin to take a truly independent position within the confines of American culture, a black position. And from that position, walk, talk, think, fight, and create, like men. Respectful of all, sharing with any, but beholden to none save our own.

"For there is hope of a tree"—this is Job talking—"if it be cut down, that it will sprout again, and that the tender branch thereof will not cease. Though the root thereof wax old in the earth, and the stock thereof die in the ground, yet through the scent of water it will bud, and bring forth boughs like a plant."

The profoundest commitment possible to a black creator in this country today—beyond all creeds, crafts, classes, and ideologies whatsoever—is to bring before his people the *scent* of freedom. He may rest assured his people will do the rest. That's what Purlie told me!

# THE SIGNIFICANCE OF
# LORRAINE HANSBERRY

Freedomways, *Third Quarter 1965*

R.D.: *Lorraine Hansberry. Articulate. Passionate. Intelligent. Young. I agree with Ossie: with her last play,* The Sign in Sidney Brustein's Window, *she showed us a sharp-sensed artist who could write about any kind of people she had a mind to. Those of us who'd been on the scene a little longer knew that some critics liked black genius "pure"—not messing around in white folks' minds and matters. Some reviews were, alas, predictable. Nonetheless, knowing Lorraine and working in* A Raisin in the Sun *remains a highlight in my life and work.*

The central problem of every Negro artist, Lorraine Hansberry included, is not only that he is estranged from his culture, but also alienated from himself. For not only has Western culture in its racist orientation an ambivalence in its expectations from Negro art, it also forces the Negro artist to be ambivalent in his relations to himself. For—Franz Boas and the science of anthropology notwithstanding—Americans, to a large degree, but not entirely, still accept race as a determinant of value; as a measure of what is good and what is less good, what is beautiful and what is less perfect, and most of all what is worthy and what is trivial. To a large degree but not entirely. If three of our young men are struck dead in freedom's cause in Mississippi, the shock of horror that shoots through the country is directly attributable to the fact that two of these sacrifices were of superior consequences to us, racially, than was the third. In our country, regardless of how they may have personally objected to it, a Mickey Schwerner and an Andy Goodman can confer status on a James Chaney merely by dying in his company. For they were white and he was black; and by sharing a death and a grave they raised him to the level of their importance—an importance he, because he was Negro, could never have achieved by dying for his freedom by himself. This realization that no matter what one does, or how well, race will always be dragged into the judging of it, will be decisive to a large degree but not entirely, must come one day sooner or later—like death—to every Negro artist.

He must then lay aside his life's work: all his tools, all his ideas and theories about the world and about himself—his artist's dreams and plannings—and wrestle mightily within himself. He must fight the whole of Western civilization within himself, trying to discover who and what he is in the light of a culture determined to avoid giving him a direct answer—that does not know whether to do with him, or to do without him—that has nowhere, just yet, to place him and his aspirations, but is afraid to leave him free to find a place for himself. And he must curse and rage and argue and fight and carry this muffled war within himself until he can, with whatever honor he has left, come to some sort of peace with the system, which he can only hope is short of total surrender. He must come to terms with the fact that in the light of Western culture he is different, maybe not permanently, but certainly as far as the human eye can see; that even in art he is a prisoner—to a large degree but not entirely—within the confines of his blackness. And that, though nobody expects him to remain in his cell forever—in fact the door is unlocked from time to time—still, nobody is prepared, or desirous, that he should come out of it . . . just yet.

Lorraine's particular prison, as is mine, was that division of the art world—of common aesthetics and public taste—bounded all too often by what Broadway and Hollywood think can be sold at a profit . . . where, to a large extent but not entirely, white is still right . . . a world which assumes almost without thinking that the good, the true, and the beautiful are eternally attributable to being white in the first place. And it is here, in this liberally persuaded, permissive, but yet reluctant, America, amidst these holier-than-thou, Anglo-Saxon assumptions mindlessly held—aristocratic intuitions of values felt at our expense—amidst these institutionalized responses, these pre-conscious judgments, subjective, privileged, and willful . . . about us, and against us: it is here that we black ones must live and love also, creating, out of our private anguish and eternal bafflement, the best art we know.

Our limits are handed down to us, like secondhand clothes, from the white man. But what else is there with which to clothe our nakedness? For not only does he set the standards by which all excellence is to be judged, he considers himself to a large degree—but not entirely—to be that standard. That he, himself, is that sweet perfection which all legitimate aspiration, artistic and otherwise, must—in the very nature of things—move upward towards. And though we blacks rebel in full against this arrogant Categorical Imperative, this white world, against which we break our fists, our heads, and sometimes our hearts, it is still the world that matters most to us. It is still a world of power, as opposed to our powerlessness; a world of life-or-death, which still, if it sees fit, confers status on Negro art and artists, raising a Lorraine Hansberry, a James Baldwin, a LeRoi Jones—as James Chaney was raised—to a level of literary importance which none of them, being Negro, could have attained by himself. In practical terms, the basic precepts of Western civilization—when Negro talent presents itself for judgment—keep shifting their grounds. And status, when finally conferred—in terms both of critical acclaim and public attention—seems almost tentative, as if something is being instinctively held back: like a white goddess trying dutifully to embrace a Negro man without flinching. Yes, sometimes the lightning strikes and we succeed, but always we are uneasy in the terms of our success, for there is nothing so galling to the human spirit as to suspect that in your best effort you have succeeded—but for the wrong reasons. Take *A Raisin in the Sun.*

*A Raisin in the Sun* was a big success on Broadway, both critically and at the box office. It won the New York Drama Critics Circle Award as the best play of the 1958–59 season, was subsequently made into a motion picture, and elevated Lorraine Hansberry to the first rank of American playwrights. The play deserved all this—the playwright deserved all this, and more. Without question! But I have a feeling that for all she got, Lorraine never got all she deserved in regards to *Raisin in the Sun*—that she got success, but that in her success she was cheated, both as a writer and as a Negro.

One of the biggest selling points about *Raisin*—filling the grapevine, riding the word-of-mouth, laying the foundation for its wide, wide acceptance—was how much the Younger family was just like any other American family. Some people were ecstatic to find that "it didn't really have to be about Negroes at all!" It was, rather, a walking, talking, living demonstration of our mythic conviction that, underneath, all of us Americans, *color-ain't-got-nothing-to-do-with-it,* are pretty much alike. People are just people, whoever they are; and all they want is a chance to be like other people. This uncritical assumption, sentimentally held by the audience, powerfully fixed in the character of the powerful mother with whom everybody could identify immediately and completely, made any other questions about the Youngers, and what living in the slums of South Side Chicago had done to them, not only irrelevant and impertinent, but also, disloyal: *Raisin* was a great American play, and Lorraine was a great American playwright because everybody who walked into the theatre saw in Lena Younger—especially as she was portrayed by Claudia McNeil—his own great American Mama. And that was decisive.

It was good for the great American audience that all of the little guilt feelings and nagging reservations that are raised inevitably by the mere prospect of having to sit through a *Negro* play could have been set so soon to rest by the simple expedient of seeing Lena Younger, and knowing she was in charge—that they could surrender themselves to her so completely, could find somebody they could trust absolutely up there on that stage—somebody so familiar to them—so comfortable. It was, I say, good for them—and certainly it was good for business. But was it—in the light of the author's real intention—good for the play? It was good that people of all colors, strata, faiths, and persuasions could identify so completely with Lena Younger and her family, and their desire to better themselves in the American way. But that's not what the play was about!

The play was about Walter Lee, Lena's son, and what happened to him as a result of having his dream, his life's ambition, endlessly frustrated by poverty and its attendant social and personal degradation. Walter Lee's dreams of "being somebody," of "making it" like everybody else, were not respectable to Mama, and not very important to us. He wanted a liquor store, which would enable him to exploit the misery of his fellow slum dwellers like they were exploited by everybody else. Walter Lee is corrupted by the materialistic aspirations at the heart of Western civilization, and his corruption is bodied forth in his petty, little dream. But it was his dream, *and it was all he had!* And that made it a matter of life or death to him, revolutionary, dangerous in its implications. For it could explode if frustrated; it could destroy people, it could kill, if frustrated! That's what Lorraine was warning us about. But we would only listen to Mama, and Mama did not ever fully understand Walter Lee! Nor the millions of panicky young Americans just like him, caught up in the revolution of rising expectations, in the midst of an affluent society that insists on playing with fire as far as these distorted dreamers are concerned: dangling unspeakable wealth before their eyes every day, yet slapping down their every attempt to reach up and grab, like everybody else. Walter Lees by the millions, most of them black, trapped in grinding poverty, hemmed in and pinned down in the ghetto, eating out their hearts waiting for the first cheap chance that comes along. But it never comes soon enough, and what is there left for the Walter Lees to do, but to explode in violence and bloodshed? This is the Walter Lorraine was concerned about, Walter of the "long, hot summers," Walter whose only way out is killing and being killed, blowing out his life in some filthy gutter! Or shooting dope into his veins!

Of course Lorraine seemed to let Walter escape from his fate into the suburbs, and by so doing to let us off the hook: we go out of the same door as Walter does. Whatever happens, Walter is still in Mama's hands, and things are just bound to work out all right. But will they? Has not Walter merely swapped one impossible dream for another? For surely Lorraine would be the last to suggest that life in the suburbs is the sufficient cure for life in the slums. For Walter belongs with the poor. Poverty is like an infectious plague, and Walter Lee is a carrier and will carry his spreading ghetto with him wherever he goes as long as he is poor.

Though *Raisin* made its name and its fame in terms of its surfaces, which seem to reflect the fairy tale of success in "the American way" at all its points, Lorraine was not a Negro for nothing. She knew that the American dream held by Mama is as unworkable in this day and age as that held by Walter. She knew that Mama's old-fashioned morality was no solution to being poor and being black in America, even in the suburbs. It's all there, implicit, in Walter and in the play. But we were too busy smiling up at Mama—loving her, blessing her, needing her—to see it.

Lorraine, I am sure, wanted very much that we should understand Walter and his warning as much as we did Mama and her reassurance. But the people who sit in judgment made their choice: Walter's dream and the threat it contained for our society ended for them when the curtain went down.* But for Lorraine, and those of us who remember, the play's intent was expressed in those lines from Langston Hughes from which she chose her title:

WHAT HAPPENS TO A DREAM DEFERRED?

Does it dry up
like a raisin in the sun?
Or fester like a sore—
And then run?
Does it stink like rotten meat?
Or crust and sugar over—
like a syrupy sweet?

Maybe it just sags
like a heavy load.

Or does it explode?

---

*It is their God-given privilege to misread us whenever they want.

Lorraine's play was meant to dramatize Langston's question, not to answer it.

But success and the great American audience decreed that Walter and his dream was Mama's problem. And that as long as she was around to straighten him out, nobody needed to worry. Lorraine accepted that success—and that verdict. What else could she do under the circumstances?

But she was to have another chance. To write another play, whose primary intent would not be short-circuited by having the audience kidnap a character, as they had done Mama, and steal her away. Next time her intent would be crystal clear, her approach absolutely straightforward. She would insist the audience listen to—and the critic respect—what she had to say in its sum and in its integrity. It was to be all or none. Take it whole, or leave it entirely: don't tamper! That's the way she wrote it, and that's the way they played it.

She called it *The Sign in Sidney Brustein's Window.* Many of us thought it her best. I'm glad she made them look at her again, before she died.

# THE WONDERFUL WORLD OF
# LAW AND ORDER*

❧

*1966*

R.D.: *Ossie always defined himself, first and foremost, as a writer, but his second passion was economics. He used to joke that if he happened to get arrested at some protest or other, he'd happily "do time" as long as he could write or read his many books on economics! As is apparent throughout this collection of some of his writings, he was deeply committed to art in service of social responsibility. His most celebrated play,* Purlie Victorious, *while a farce, was in fact a most serious examination of the insidious economic underpinnings of racism in all its cultural, psychological, and social manifestations.*

The Negro in this country has to write protest, because he is a protestant. He can't help but be. He cannot accept the situation in which he finds himself, so, therefore, he is driven to scream out against the oppression that surrounds him, that suffocates him. So that what he writes will be in the nature of protest. The protest has been, and still is and must continue to be, loud, bitter, and haranguing. It must irritate. It must shake. It must disturb. It must move the very bowels of compassion. It must be angry. It must be aimed at corrective action and now.

---

*An abridged version of an essay first published in *Anger, and Beyond: The Negro Writer in the United States,* edited by Herbert Hill (HarperCollins, 1966).

But those are not the limits of protest, and I have chosen to approach the whole problem from another direction. I say that we can protest about an unjust situation on an intellectual level by saying that in addition to being unjust the situation is also ridiculous, and that we can show that it is ridiculous, and perhaps even laughable, and, therefore, not worthy of the behavior of educated, culturally advanced human beings, such as must be the kind of people, both white and black, who inhabit America at this late date.

I have chosen to make my protest in the form of revealing the ridiculous institutions that have brought us, in our national life, to a very critical point in our cultural, economic, political, and social history. The theatre, as you know, has long been given to pointing the finger of ridicule at that which it found to be ridiculous. I can imagine no other institution on the face of the earth more ridiculous than the institution of segregation, and, though it is cruel, though it is capable of committing murder and destroying me and oppressing me physically and brutally, emasculating me, still, there is a possibility that I can maintain enough of my own balance and point of view to say that in addition to being oppressive and in addition to killing me it is also absolutely ridiculous.

One of the traditions by which my people have been able to survive in the oppressive atmosphere of American culture has been the tradition of corrective and educational humor. We told jokes, one to another, but we weren't telling jokes for the sake of getting off fast quips and gags. That stream of humor had to carry our sense of self, our sense of history, our hope for the future, our religious concern about man's relationship to man. It had to point us to the future and tell us to "Wait, bide your time. The day is coming when you can stand up and be a man." I would like to give back to the Negro people the humor they themselves created, give it back in the form in which they created it and let it begin, once again, to serve the function for which it was originally created.

There was a man, who has become synonymous with some of the aspects of our trouble, named Stepin Fetchit. Now, we know that Stepin Fetchit was earning a living; he almost made himself a rich man by caricaturing a certain attitude about Negro people which we know not to be true but which certain people wanted to believe, and this idea was that all Negroes were lazy and stupid and they drawled and said, "Yowsah."

This man was, perhaps, not very bright, and he became a good stereotypical justification of what was wrong with Negroes and why they lived in ghettoes and why they'd never make it. Because they just didn't have it. They were all shiftless. They were all lazy. And they never thought for themselves and always waited for somebody to do something for them. On this basis, we rightly protested the use of Mr. Stepin Fetchit and his character and his talent to demean the whole Negro race, because we realized that the community about us was drawing conclusions from his behavior which we knew to be incorrect and using his behavior to justify the continued oppression in which we found ourselves.

But let's look a little deeper into what originally was behind the meaning of Stepin Fetchit's lazy character. As you will remember, those of you who have a long memory, we were slaves in this country, and we were required to work from sunup to sundown and there was no time off, no coffee breaks, no Social Security, none of the few benefits that we have only lately acquired. Slavery was straight labor, even above and beyond the devotion required of a mule. And we were required, for the benefit of our masters, to work ourselves, literally, to death. If you could—if you were an honest man, an honest Negro, and if you had no way to escape—you would literally work yourself to death, because it was cheaper for a master to work a slave to death, to get all the work out of him and later buy a replacement.

Now, a slave like Stepin Fetchit—who really was a smart man, who understood the ways of the white folks—would suddenly discover that he was regarded as a very unintelligent creature. So when the master would send him to get a rope he would come back with maybe a plow, until finally the slave owner would get the idea that this man was so dumb and so inefficient and so shiftless that nothing could be done but to let him sit under a tree.

You might ask why. Why didn't the man take Stepin Fetchit and sell him or get rid of him? Because unconsciously this behavior identified, confirmed, and reinforced the slave owner's prejudices against the possibility of Negroes being responsible, thoughtful, and efficient people. So that the Negro achieved two purposes. He saved himself by being too dumb to do the work that the mules and the other slaves were doing, and therefore he survived. And he also gave the overlord the satisfaction of believing that all Negroes were dumb and lazy.

However, I must now protest against the wrong, the invalid use of a stereotype, by whites or by others, after it has been disembodied and the protest content has been removed. Most of the stereotypes we know about Negroes were invented by Negroes for the purposes of survival and social correction. We do this all the time. It is a way in which a society tries to control its members. It will criticize its leaders. It will state its aims, through stereotypes, through jokes and humor. But our humor has been taken away, emptied of its bitter protest content, and has been used against us. And this has led us, sometimes, to rebel against our own humor.

In my play *Purlie Victorious* I have tried to restore the protest content of the Negro's humor. I attempted to comment upon the world of law and order, especially in a particular scene.

It is the second scene of the play, and it takes place in the commissary. The commissary is a place on the cotton patch where the man who owns the cotton patch sells food and seed and goods to the people who work the cotton patch for him. He sells these things at such an exorbitant price that no matter how hard you work on the farm you will never be able to pay the bill, and until you can pay the bill you can't leave. Therefore, this is an arrangement which ensures him a permanent supply of cheap labor, and his instrument of control is the company store, the commissary.

Now, our hero is Old Captain Cotchipee, who represents the old, unreconstructed South. He has a benevolent attitude toward "his" Negro people, as you will understand, but he has a son, young Charlie Cotchipee, who is our hope in the white liberal community in the South and in the North, and I think you will recognize some of his possibilities and his great limitations in the character as we see him.

Charlie Cotchipee has been brought up, subversively, by the Negro woman who runs the house. She has taught Charlie Cotchipee to revere Abraham Lincoln. This immediately throws him into a tremendous disturbance, because he has been taught the value of freedom and dignity and he has to live in the South where these values are denied. So right away our young liberal is in hot water.

Now, into the scene comes the greatest stereotype of them all, "Uncle Tom." I called him Gitlow, because the question arises, "How low can you git?" The answer: "Git low!" We at first recognize Gitlow as a man who is a masterful Uncle Tom, but as the scene goes along, I think we will understand a little bit more of what Gitlow really is all about.

I offer this brief scene, which is not entitled in the play "The World of Law and Order" but which is basically concerned with the world of law and order. It was taken from *Purlie Victorious* or *A Non-Confederate Romp Through the Cotton Patch*.

OLD CAPTAIN: Yes sirree. He told the boys over at Ben's Bar in town that he was all for mixing the races together . . . He says white children and darkey children ought to go to the same schoolhouse together.

GITLOW: Well, tell me the truth!

OLD CAPTAIN: He got hisself so worked up, somebody had to cool him down with a Coca-Cola bottle.

GITLOW: Tell me the truth again.

CHARLIE: Now, that wasn't what I said.

OLD CAPTAIN: You callin' me a liar, boy?

CHARLIE: No, sir, but I just said that since it was the law of the land—

OLD CAPTAIN: It is not the law of the land. No such a thing.

CHARLIE: I didn't think it would do any harm if they went to school together. That's all.

OLD CAPTAIN: I know. That's enough.

CHARLIE: Well, they do it up North.

OLD CAPTAIN: Why, this is down South. And down here they'll go to school together over me and Gitlow's dead body. Right, Git?

GITLOW: You the boss, boss.

CHARLIE: *(Still pressing the liberal point of view.)* But this is the law of the land.

OLD CAPTAIN: Never mind the law, boy. Look here. You like old Gitlow? Hm? You trust him? You always did, didn't you?

CHARLIE: Yes, sir.

OLD CAPTAIN: And Gitlow here—why, he would cut off his right arm for you if you was to ask him. Wouldn't you, Git?

GITLOW: You the boss, boss.

OLD CAPTAIN: Now, Gitlow—Gitlow ain't nothing if he ain't a Negro. Ain't you, Git?

GITLOW: Oh, two-three hundred percent I calculate.

OLD CAPTAIN: Now, if you really want to know what the Nigra thinks about this here integration and all the like of that, don't ask the Supreme Court. Ask Gitlow. Go ahead. Ask him.

CHARLIE: *(Knowing where this is going to lead.)* I don't need to ask him.

OLD CAPTAIN: Then I'll ask him. Raise your right hand, Git.

*(GITLOW raises his right hand.)* Do you solemnly swear to tell the truth, the whole truth, nothing but the truth, so help you God?

GITLOW: I do.

OLD CAPTAIN: Gitlow, as God is your judge and maker, do you believe in your heart that God intended white folks and Nigra children to go to school together?

GITLOW: No, sir. I do not.

OLD CAPTAIN: Do you, so help you God, think that white folks and black should mix and associate in streetcars, buses and railway stations, in any way, shape, form or fashion?

GITLOW: Absolutely not.

OLD CAPTAIN: And is it not your considered opinion—God strike you dead if you lie—that all my Negroes are happy with things in the Southland just the way they are?

GITLOW: Indeed, I do.

OLD CAPTAIN: Do you think ary a single darkey on my place would ever think of changing a single thing about the South? And to hell with the Supreme Court, as God is your judge and maker?

GITLOW: As God is my judge and maker and you are my boss, I do not.

OLD CAPTAIN: *(Turns to CHARLIE.)* The voice of the Negro himself. What more proof do you want, boy?

CHARLIE: I don't care whose voice it is. It's still the law of the land and I intend to obey it.

OLD CAPTAIN: *(This is more than he can take.)* Get out of my place, boy. Get out of my place before I kill you out. I'll kill you. I'll kill you. *(He is so carried away that he has an apoplectic fit.)*

GITLOW: *(Seeing his source of economic security about to vanish.)* Easy. Easy, Captain. Easy. Easy. *(OLD CAPTAIN groans. GIT-LOW sets him in the rocking chair and goes to the shelf and picks up a few little bottles.)* Some aspirin, sir . . . ?

OLD CAPTAIN: Why can't he see what they doing to the South-land, Gitlow? Why can't he see it like you and me? If there is one responsibility you've got, boy, above all others, I said to him, it is these Nigras. Your Nigras, boy. Good, honest, hard-working cotton choppers, if you keep after them.

GITLOW: Yes, Lord.

OLD CAPTAIN: Something between you and them, boy, no Supreme Court in the world can understand. If it wasn't for me, they'd starve to death. What's gonna become of them, boy? After I'm gone.

GITLOW: *(Looks to heaven.)* That's a good question, Lawd. You answer.

OLD CAPTAIN: They belong to you, boy. To you. Every one of them. My old Confederate father told me on his deathbed, "Feed the Nigras first, after the horses and cattle." And I've done it every time.

*(GITLOW continues to sing.)*

OLD CAPTAIN: *(Being soothed back into the state of spiritual grace.)* Ah, Gitlow. Old friend. There is something ab-solutely sacred about that spiritual. I live for the day you will sing that thing over my grave.

GITLOW: Me, too, old Captain. Me, too.

I have tried in that scene to sketch broadly what I knew to be the psychological and personal truths of the lives of many people and what I knew were the economic and social foundations against which those lives had, necessarily, to be lived.

Each actor, each human being, you will notice, is caught up in a role, in a stereotype, and he behaves in accord with that stereotype. Now, I have tried to put in the stereotype what I know to be the truth of the situation out of which the stereotype grew in the first place, and I am happy to say that I think I have succeeded.

But these were not stereotypes that I created. They were created a long time ago on the plantations and then were taken by white-faced minstrels and emptied of their ammunition and protest and bite and made into something altogether different. I merely tried to bring them back where they belong.

But what is my larger intent? Is it merely to show you that we can laugh? That we look at the situations of life with more than angry eyes?

No. I have a specific reason for writing a play like *Purlie Victorious* in the manner in which it was written. My intent was to have a handbook of consolation, information, and struggle, which my people and their friends could use to understand, explain the situation in which they found themselves, and point the way toward a possible solution.

This particular play was situated in the South, where the Negro is in economic servitude on a plantation. Another kind of play needs to be written about the Negro in Harlem, who is in a different kind of servitude, but nonetheless real and nonetheless disturbing and about which something must be done. That play could be done with humor, and it could point to the same kind of moral and teach the same kind of lesson in the same kind of way. For it is equally ridiculous that people live in slums in this day and age of automation, when we have in our power all that it takes to create better housing and decent communities. It's ridiculous, in addition to everything else it is, that people are required to live in rat-infested decaying slum houses.

But to turn again to *Purlie Victorious* . . . If you'll recall, in the scene between Old Captain and Gitlow and Charlie, Old Captain was defending what was, to him, ordained by God. He believed that anyone who attempted to change the world of law and order, this peaceful ordained relationship between the two groups, was threatening the very foundations of civilization. Because Old Captain believed, as quite a few of us believe, white liberals and black liberals, that law and order is the essence of civilization.

But this is not necessarily true. Justice is the essence of civilization, and when law and order is imposed upon a basically unjust situation there is bound to be a clash, sooner or later, between law and order—no matter how respectably law and order is presented and preserved—and those forces whose cry and need for justice makes them unable to maintain a real respect for law and order.

I do not say that I have been liberated from all respect for law and order. On the contrary, I realize what chaotic conditions could come about if the skeins of law and order were to vanish, if violence and brute force were the only resort to settling our disputes.

I know what would happen. I really want law and order, but I realize that law and order presuppose justice. When we speak of young people in the streets of Harlem as having no respect for policemen, we must remember that the policemen had no respect for those young people in the first place. And when we describe young people as "punks" or "hoodlums"—words I hate to use; I don't use those kinds of words because it gives permission for a policeman to shoot a human being and forget that he is a human being—who loot, break stores open, and rob jewelry and socks and underwear and garments—and we deplore these things—let us not forget the other looting that goes on silently and quietly, even on the level of the policeman, who, at a certain time every week, goes to a certain store or apartment and picks up a brown paper bag filled with money.

Who is the more successful of the looters, those unfortunate young people who were out on the streets of dismal cities on hot August nights or the policeman who has, for years, made it in a middle-class society by looting every day in the black community, by turning his back on dope, by turning his back on gambling and prostitution, by not insisting upon the preservation of even the most basic rights for the members of that community? I think one should know where the looting began in the first place.

If there is to be respect for law and order, it must be based upon mutual understanding and a respect for those who are under the law, and order must be maintained for the benefit of all of those who are under the law.

We face a great crisis in our country today. We have been called upon by some of our leaders to refrain from demonstrations and protest because they might be construed as an attack upon law and order. We are told that attacks on law and order might give ammunition to the white backlash, and there are those who think that this is the greatest harm that could come to the cause of the Negro people.

Now this is a debatable point. I am forced to ask, if there is a white backlash, what is it lashing back from? Where was it all the time? Am I sure that those who are lashing back were not waiting for someone to come along and give them an excuse to lash back?

I am not so certain. I fear greatly that the Negro people, after mounting a magnificent struggle for their freedom, as they have done so often in the past, will be asked, once again, in the name of some vague larger freedom, in the name of the larger community, in the name of law and order, to halt their struggle and, once again, we'll come out of that struggle, as I personally came out of World War II, to find that we have lost the war that we thought we had won. And I would hope that those who ask for patience, those who ask us to wait will meet us with a real concrete program of action, with real remedies, so we will have something to be patient about, something to wait for, something that we can understand and appreciate and explain to ourselves and our children.

We wait now, at the darkest hour of the night, in order to make it peaceable and to prepare ourselves better for the action which is certain to come at dawn.

# RE: A NEW CONSTITUTION

~

*c. 1968*

R.D.: *Ossie would often mention that the Constitution was written to serve people who had come to America (displacing the Native Americans and whoever else was here) to escape the tyrannies of Europe and to search for personal liberty without burdensome taxes. Fast forward. Individual merchants began to band together as companies. Companies became corporations became conglomerates, which eventually co-opted the power and privilege of the citizen. We are fast becoming the United States of Corporate America. We need a new Constitutional Convention to acknowledge the trend and to decide what kind of America we are or shall become.*

More and more I have come to believe that even if half the candidates were geniuses and the other half angels, this election cannot save us. We need something more now—certainly since Robert Kennedy and Martin Luther King, Jr., are dead and the outsiders, growing ever larger in number, are feeling more left out than ever. We need something more, something touching us all much more deeply than this election can possibly do.

We need a new mandate, newly arrived at, a new definition of our America. Forget the elections; it is too late for them to save us. Let's call instead for a second Constitutional Convention like the first one in 1787 by which we still try to live, but which now no longer meets our needs.

The first Constitution was called, by William Gladstone, the grandest document ever struck off by the mind of man. The fact of the matter is that the first Constitution began as a compromise. No Negroes were there at its writing; no women; no poor people; no Mexican-Americans; no Puerto Ricans; no American Indians; and, most of all, no young people as we know them today.

It could be that the only political gesture worthy of us in the crisis we face would be to suspend the elections and call instead for a new constitutional convention, a new set of rules by which to govern ourselves—an up-to-date set of rules which we could all participate in formulating. Everybody would have a chance to speak up about the kind of constitution he wanted—which means that everyone would be forced to spell out the kind of America he wanted. Participatory democracy would be given its first great chance.

The old Founding Fathers were, I'm sure, all honorable men, but they most certainly did not represent me. Let us seek out from among ourselves a new set of Founding Fathers, and this time let us include all those people not now truly represented in the councils of our nation. A new constitutional convention where all the groups in our country can converge, confront, and hammer out a new country—one that will put first things first, that will establish a new set of priorities, and surely a debate among all the contending groups about fundamentals as jarring, as shocking, as disruptive as it might be, would be less bloody, less fiery, less expensive than the other kind of revolution—the kind with bullets.

Let us sit down now and negotiate a peace treaty among ourselves. Our country is our destiny. We can control both, but only if we are prepared to risk the dangers of real democracy. Forget the elections. Let's call for a constitutional convention. The First Republic of the United States of America is dead. Long live the Second Republic.

# ON ECONOMICS

～

*1968*

R.D.: *While Ossie was filming* Sam Whiskey *with Burt Reynolds and Clint Walker, the publicity people at Levy-Gardner-Laven and United Artists arranged for him to be interviewed for the* New York Times *and the* Los Angeles Times. *Somehow, the subject turned from cowboy westerns to economics. Ossie was asked to explain his fascination with economics for an in-depth piece. We came across this draft in our archives. I don't know if it ever made it to the papers.*

M ost history books say America was settled by people in search of various freedoms.

Actually, the main motive was economic, and certainly the black people came as items of commerce. It doesn't seem possible to make sense of American history unless you study the dollars and cents of it.

Columbus was looking for India and its spices so people could make money selling spices. White Christians went to Africa and took millions of Africans as slaves—not because they were mean, but because there was a decent buck in it. Morality usually affects man's behavior long after the fact.

We congratulate ourselves on the progress of liberty in

human society, and we're happy that we're so enlightened and that slavery has been outlawed over most of the space of the civilized globe.

We say this testifies to man's moral improvement.

It does no such thing. It merely means that machine labor has outmoded human labor. The real reason we've abolished slavery is because machine labor is more economical than slave labor.

There was a time in this country when we were on the verge of abolishing slave labor, but then Eli Whitney invented the cotton gin. The cotton gin made the production of cotton economical and it was this fact that accounts for the fact that slavery wasn't abolished, but went on to become the dominant mode of production in our country. The Negro presence in America at all is tied up directly to that fact.

Even after emancipation, when slave labor was abolished, the Negro's place in the American society was determined by the fact that he was a reservoir of cheap labor in the North and in the South.

This state of affairs roughly has continued until a few years ago when machines were perfected which could do the dirty work cheaper and more efficiently than even Negroes could.

Two years ago ninety-five percent of all cotton picked in Mississippi was picked by machines. You've only to remember that it was to pick that cotton in the first place that black men were brought to this country. He's been tied to that cotton politically, economically, and socially for generations. It shouldn't be difficult to realize what a threat the cotton-picking machine posts to black people.

Next time you step into an elevator and push a button, remember you've pushed a black man out of a job that used to be his almost by right.

According to Bureau of Statistics figures, three out of four jobs held by Negro people fall within the category of unskilled labor. These three out of four jobs are the natural target of automation, which already, according to some experts, is removing each week from 30,000 to 40,000 jobs in the unskilled category from the American economy.

It is the black man's response to this economic disaster in which he and his family are caught that creates the thrust in the current rebellion in the black community.

If America is a prison for the black man, it was made so basically by economics. And only an understanding of economics will provide a key to his liberation.

The tragedy of the black man is that he has no power to control the economic facts of his life. The tragedy of the white man is that he does not understand that the economic tragedy that has blasted the black community, in less than ten years' time will also blast the white community. Then, because America refuses to understand economics, she will search for a way out of her economic dilemma, possibly by looking for scapegoats rather than for basic solutions. What will make a better target than twenty to thirty million black people marching up and down the streets talking about how hungry and unhappy they are?

America has long since solved the problem of production of goods and services. Every year our gross national product soars higher and higher. It will soon be one trillion dollars annually. But in 1929 we discovered production was not the answer. Distribution is the weak link in our economic chain. We have done nothing fundamental to solve the problem of distribution since 1929. Government handouts, WPA, poverty programs, food stamps, subsidized agriculture—none of these can or will solve the problem. A war that is being lost, a gold reserve rapidly disappearing, an ever-growing number of the poor and dispossessed in our society, people who no longer account for anything in our society either as producers or consumers, with every year more and more goods being produced by fewer and fewer workers—all these economic factors are moving with horrifying speed toward crisis.

With an understanding of economics we might solve these problems, for indeed they are all soluble.

But this mighty country, caught up in a frenzy of racism, mesmerized by the fear it is somehow being contaminated by millions of unneeded—and therefore unwanted—black people, is hardly in the position to deal rationally with economics.

It is far easier to think not of dollars and cents, but of "niggers," and under cover of our fears do all the horrible things to our darker minorities that we are so wont to chastise the rest of the world for doing.

If I had it to do all over again, you're damn right I would study economics. I believe it is the only way out.

# A 35-MILLIMETER TALKING DRUM*

The New York Times, *September 20, 1970*

I went to Africa to direct a film, *Kongi's Harvest*, written by Wole Soyinka, Nigeria's world-famous playwright, who had just been released after two years in prison. The civil war was over, but the tragedy was heavy on my conscience and I went in order to become in my own way an open and avowed enemy of the white Western Judeo-Christian capitalist civilization that had caused it. Africa is not free—not yet—and is therefore not herself: she is imprisoned still by white imperial necessities, which dare not let her go.

Now, after 350 years I had come back—not with a gun but a camera—to do what best I could to set things right: to make Wole's film. But revolutions if they are to succeed must start quietly—in the beginning nobody must know you are there. *Kongi's Harvest* is on the surface not revolutionary at all; it is the happening conflict between the old and the new taking place all over Africa today. The white man is not present, and is in fact seldom mentioned, and it will seem on first look that nothing in *Kongi's Harvest* represents a threat to white power and its interests on the African continent. But wait—let me run it down for you—then look again.

---

*Publication title: "When Is a Camera a Weapon?"

It didn't start this way for me, although the venture was in-deed unique back in 1967 when I first got involved. It was enough for me then that *Kongi's Harvest* was to be the first major motion picture produced on the African continent by an African film company: an African story by an African writer, to be filmed in an African setting not only for African audiences—which are quite considerable—but also for audiences all over the world. They, the Africans themselves, wanted to start their own film industry and wanted me, an Afro-American, to come over and direct their first feature. I jumped at the chance.

They (by "they" I really mean Francis Oladele, who is a whole film company disguised as one man)—they had the stories, they had the actors, they had the locations—they even had some of the money. Of course, they did not as yet have technical facilities: stu-dios for interiors, film labs for processing—no cameras, sound equipment of their own, etc. (But these things can be rented.)

The most important thing they did not have in Nigeria was technicians—black film technicians with the necessary skills to shoot a motion picture and then put it together. But this is what excited me most of all. For here, in America, we have such people, black film technicians with as much savvy and talent (but not as much experience) as the whites—black producers, black direc-tors, black cinematographers, black sound men, editors, scenic artists, grips, carpenters, costume designers, the lot—as perfectly capable as are whites to do everything that goes into the making of a modern motion picture, but who, thanks to rampant racism in the craft unions which largely exclude blacks, Puerto Ricans, and other minorities, cannot find jobs in their own country!

Where else in the world, I thought, could Africa better satisfy her need for first-class filmmaking talent than right here in black America, from among her own lost children still looked upon by white Western civilization as rejects and misfits? Black hands across the white man's cold and frozen ocean! Men of African descent from both sides of the ocean helping each other to get a new thing going, a black thing, in the world of motion pictures—the answer to one of my fondest dreams. I would have done it for nothing plus expenses!

But war came to Nigeria, Wole went off to prison, and it was not until 1969, two years and a civil war later, when I was directing *Cotton Comes to Harlem* for Sam Goldwyn, Jr., that Francis Oladele was able to begin putting *Kongi's Harvest* together again. He brought in Arthur DuBow of Herald Productions (*Putney Swope*) for a third on the provision that he raise the funds; Lennart Berns of Omega Films, a Swedish company, came in for a third—he was to furnish the crew, the equipment, and all technical facilities; Francis Oladele and Calpenny Nigeria Films Ltd., for their third, were to provide script, director, cast, costumes, locations, and accommodations. Unfortunately, in light of the deal with the Swedish company, my own dream of taking over an all Afro-American crew had to be deferred. But thanks to Cliff Frazier of the Community Film Workshop Council, and the Institute of International Education, the John and Mary R. Markle Foundation, and the Ford Foundation, I was able to take Sam Holmes, Karma Stanley, and Charles Lewis over as my assistants: only three—but it was a start.

And certainly there was enough before me to get excited about: an African story adapted for the screen from his own play by Wole Soyinka; Soyinka himself, now freed from prison, acting the title role of Kongi the dictator; and me, Ossie Davis, black, ambitious, three hundred years removed from these shores, yet back again looking for the umbilical—a way to authenticate the fact that, in spite of all, I, too, was an African.

So it was that at 7:30 A.M., Sunday, March 1, 1970, I found myself outside an imposing government building in Ibadan, Nigeria—our first location—getting set for my first shot. The crew was ready (with a Swedish crew, getting set doesn't take much time—even their mistakes are faster), the cast was ready, but some of the motorcycles we had borrowed from the army were acting up, and some of the cars we needed for the procession had not showed yet. But I was not nervous; I am a patient man, and besides, such foul-ups are always a part of getting the first shot in the can—ask any director. And as always, I had a head full of unfinished thoughts to sustain me. I could wait.

Thoughts about revolution, about black liberation, for that was the ultimate meaning of what I was engaged in: how to change the world from what I hated, to what I could love. Black Africa is much quieter than Vietnam, but the struggle going on there is vicious nonetheless, and speaks much louder to the Western world. White Western Judeo-Christian capitalist civilization might continue to exist in its present form if—in spite of Mr. Nixon—it "loses" Southeast Asia; it would be staggered, but not knocked out if—to the chagrin of Mr. Rockefeller—it also "lost" South America. But without Africa's rich oil and mineral resources to sustain her industry, Western civilization becomes economically impossible: it will fall. It must continue to control access to Africa's raw material—and such is colonialism, however you may disguise it—or it is dead!

Europe and America, with their tremendous investments to protect and to defend, know this. Africa, all too often, does not. Hence there is yet a semblance of "peace" for the white man on the African continent. A "peace" made possible only by Africa's weakness and self-division. But weakness is relative and self-division is not everlasting. Self-knowledge in this instance is the first step in the cure for them both. To free herself, Africa must first know herself. But how? To free herself, she must convert self-knowledge into unity—a oneness of purpose, a determination to engage the enemy in common struggle, a common consciousness, an African sense of self, achieved in the face of many differences in language, custom, culture, and religion—a unity without which Africa must forever remain at the feet of Europe and America.

Unity, indeed, but how? Surely film can help, I said to myself, daring to think the unthinkable as I waited. Surely film might be one method, one of many—small at first, but potentially most powerful—by which Africans might begin to construct the new language, the new way of talking, first to themselves, then to each other, and finally, to the world.

A camera is not a gun, but surely it is first cousin to the drum—the drum which since time immemorial has been a main means of African communication among the tribes. A camera cannot decide the issues, but it can certainly have influence on those who do. Why should not this film, this *Kongi's Harvest*, be one of the new but necessary insights into themselves and into their own values that Africans cry for?

Why can we not begin here—with this camera, this crew, this cast of Africans, this story—and *this* director—begin here in this place and on this day (the power of the thought was making me drunk) the spiritual self-reconstruction of all Africa! The call of the Mother summoning her parts and her powers for a final once-and-for-all confrontation with white Western Judeo-Christian capitalist civilization! Power grows out of the barrel of a gun, it is said; but might not power also grow, in this instance, out of the barrel of a camera! I tasted the forbidden thought, and because it was sweet, I trembled.

Somebody touched me.

It was eight o'clock, the sun was high, and already we were thirty minutes behind schedule. I listened as Tunde, my valuable African assistant, gave the cast my last-minute instructions in English and in Yoruba, and turned as Christel, the script girl, did the same in Swedish to the crew—Swedes, damn good, the best I've ever seen, whom I would get to know and to appreciate more as we went along. Next time, the crew would be black—Africans and Afro-Americans—that's still a big dream of mine. But this time? Well, in film as in life, a revolution has to start where it can—

I called the question:

"Ready, Bo?" I said to my sound man.

"Ready."

"Ready, Lasse?" to my camera operator.

"Ready."

I looked around, trying to stop feeling too damn small for the occasion, and said, in one of my better voices:

"Roll 'em!"

And that's what we did.

# THE NATURE OF THE REVOLUTION

Stand By!, *May–June 1971*

We are all concerned about what is happening in our country—concerned about what we can and must do to survive as a nation. Now, for *Stand By!* readers, let me deal specifically with broadcasting and the black revolution.

Revolutions are not about color. Revolutions are about power. The transfer of power from a group that has too much to a group that hasn't got enough constitutes a revolution. In an orderly society the transfer is accomplished through law and order, peace and decency. Those who need the opportunities find ways legally, orderly, morally, to satisfy those needs. But when law and order doesn't work, or when it was intended not to work in the first place, then power must be transferred by other means, means that often lead to fire, death, and perhaps destruction of that powerful society.

Consider how the system operates to exclude me, to keep me weak and helpless while demanding my allegiance, demanding that I feed into the system, demanding my obedience, demanding my willingness to do more than my share even to qualify for the crumbs that fall off democracy's tables.

We have a racial crisis, true, but I dare say that the racial crisis in our country is one-third of the iceberg that might wreck us. I'm talking about jobs, not about race, I'm talking about jobs that we need, want, and must have. We are in the process of trying to get these jobs by peaceful means. Discussions, luncheons, talks, debates, forums, all of these methods are being used. But I say to you as a man and as a citizen that if these means do not work, then other means of solving the problems, which are far more destructive, are just on the horizon. Power! *Power* is what we are talking about. Power that jobs can bring. In a recent issue of *The Nation* magazine, an article entitled "The Wired Nation" refers to cable TV. The article says that

> Cable TV has proved to be immensely popular. By last June, 2321 systems were operating in the United States, with another 2003 under construction. An additional 2370 applications for franchises were pending before the city fathers at some 1300 cities, towns and communities. In recent years the number of subscribers has grown at a rate of 20 to 25 per cent annually, and the system now serves 12 million people, about 6 per cent of the population. Investment in CATV plants exceeds $500 million and is soaring. Estimated annual revenues of the industry are in excess of $300 million and also rising fast. Irving Kahn, President of Teleprompter Corporation, one of the companies franchised to build cable systems in Manhattan, predicts that within 10 years, 85 per cent of TV reception in the United States will be by cable.

What I am interested in is what cable TV is going to do for the black man. I want to know who will run it, who will supervise it, and who will *benefit*? Cable TV is a new opportunity for those seeking their fair share of power, and the black man must do, *at the beginning,* what he has failed to do in the past—get in at the beginning. Whenever the communications industry took a step forward in the past, the black man always came too late to be meaningfully included. When radio came into being, we didn't get in. When television arrived, the fight between AFTRA and SAG for control overshadowed problems faced by black people, so, of course, we were once again left out.

An industry gets started *not* on the basis of high ideals, *not* on the basis of communicating truths, but rather when a sufficient number of hard-headed businessmen smell an additional buck to be made. Cable television is the next ground where communications giants are going to stampede. Cable television will in ten years serve 85 percent of the needs for television in our country. The cable TV industry must soon bargain for the specialized labor needed within the industry. When some unions deal with the broadcasters, they bargain for people who are *already there.* They set standards of employment which are *already* racially exclusive. Will blacks and Puerto Ricans once again come knocking on the door to ask for a little piece *after* the deals are made? the contract signed? No!

This time, it's another ball game. Black folks are going to be there at the very inception, and we are going to shout and scream and raise hell—whatever it takes—we are going to be included!

Those in power would be wise to consider using that power responsibly. The unions' role is understandable! They are committed to creating and maintaining the best employment opportunity for their members.

But if some organizations (and I do not number AFTRA among them), because of past policy for which none of us is responsible, have handed down a membership which traditionally excludes blacks, Puerto Ricans, and other minorities, we have either to insist that those organizations change their membership rolls or have management insist that it will have a policy of open hiring. Otherwise the consequence will be confrontation at its most brute level.

Young blacks, perennial victims of America's economic dislocation, will no longer abide by the rules laid down by white and black liberals. They're not going to listen to me or to you, to anybody, but will spend their energy—and their lives—seeing to it that the rest of us won't have much of a way of life either.

As long as unions and management resort to power tactics, don't delude yourselves that minority groups are too naive to employ similar methods. Do not fool yourselves that the black folks are so kind and so gentle, so loving that they have not begun to understand how power is wielded in this country. And do not believe that because blacks do not have money, or prestige, or the kind of education other Americans have that they do not have power within their own structure.

There was something that happened in our country ten years ago that has been most instructive to black people and should be a lesson to all of us today. A young man from Boston became our country's first Catholic president. It is not so foolish to assume that schoolchildren were told that the reason he was elected president was because he believed in George Washington, that he never told lies, and that he was clean, upright, and an honest American of shiny face and lovely speech—because we thought of him as the most noble example of American youth and tradition, we elected him president of the United States.

That is a lie: it didn't happen that way at all.

How did it happen? It happened because John F. Kennedy's grandfather got to be the first Irish mayor of Boston, and not by presenting himself to the white Anglo-Saxon successful Protestants of Boston. He achieved political prominence by pulling together all Boston Irish as a power bloc so that he could confront the other power bloc. John F. Kennedy's grandfather did become the mayor of Boston. And if he had not been, JFK would never have become our president. One hundred years ago the Irish were niggers. They had it tough, were treated badly. So the Irish, as for example the Molly Maguires, went into the coal mines and blew up things. They could be called the White Panthers of their day.

The biggest riot we ever had in our country was not an explosion of black people. It was the riot of 1863 when the Irish broke loose in New York City and nearly 1,200 people were killed. They were tired of being treated like niggers and set out to burn the whole city down. It was not ethical, but that violent action changed the attitude of New York City and the whole country toward the Irish.

The economy no longer needs unskilled labor, Irish or Negro or Puerto Rican. So we are determined to acquire those skills which our highly mechanized economy does require.

And we intend to sell those skills in the marketplace like you do, without let or hindrance. Don't let us then have to change the communications industry against its will. Let it be enough that we can learn, have learned, and are willing to learn, and that we do mean business. And we mean business because it is our right and our duty to be serious about the life we live.

I appeal to management, I appeal to labor, and I appeal to blacks and Puerto Ricans. We must get together and talk power. Never mind the brotherhood: let's put our cards on the table and bargain . . . you give me that, I'll give you this. Let us confront each other while the channels of communication are still open.

Confrontations need not mean bricks and broken heads and bottles thrown. Confrontation can be the stage in which men honestly sit down, look each other in the eye, and talk turkey, and that's all. That's all the blacks and Puerto Ricans want from you who have the power.

You have power; we have power. It behooves us all to get together now and use that power responsibly—while there is still time.

# CHALLENGE FOR THE YEAR 2000

The Nation, *July 24–31, 1989*

> *The curse of poverty has no justification in our age. It is*
> *socially as cruel and blind as the practice of cannibalism*
> *at the dawn of civilization . . . The time has come for us*
> *to civilize ourselves by the total direct and immediate*
> *abolition of poverty.*
> —MARTIN LUTHER KING, JR.
> *WHERE DO WE GO FROM HERE: CHAOS OR COMMUNITY?*

Symbols and myths—when emerging uncorrupted from human experience—are precious. Then it is the poetic voice and vision that informs and infuses—the poet-warrior's, the prophet-seer's, the dreamer's—reassuring us that truth is as real as falsehood. And ultimately stronger.

In *Chaos or Community?* (published one year before his death), King's was one such voice, which drew upon another to illustrate the debilitating toll of white oppression on black children. The words upon which King drew came from the pen of W.E.B. Du Bois in manifestation of that great poet-scholar's extraordinary ability to evoke stunning images powerful enough to strike deep into our souls.

"It is difficult," Dr. Du Bois writes in his autobiographical *Dusk of Dawn,* "to let others see the full psychological meaning of caste segregation":

It is as though one, looking out from a dark cave in a side of an impending mountain, sees the world passing and speaks to it: speaks courteously and persuasively, showing them how the entombed souls are hindered in their natural movement, expression, and development: and how their loosening from prison would be a matter not simply of courtesy, sympathy, and help to them, but to all the world.

One talks on evenly and logically in this way but notices that the passing throng does not even turn its head, or if it does, glances curiously and walks on. It gradually penetrates the minds of the prisoners that the people passing do not hear; that some thick sheet of invisible but horribly tangible plate glass is between them and the world . . . Then the people within may become hysterical. They may scream and hurl themselves against the barriers, hardly realizing in their bewilderment that they are screaming in a vacuum unheard and that their antics may actually seem funny to those outside looking in. They may even, here and there, break through in blood and disfigurement, and find themselves faced by a horrified, implacable, and quite overwhelming mob of people frightened for their very own existence.

In 1967, King drew on Du Bois's 1940 analogy of the cave as background to his own tale of the months he spent living and working in the ghettos of Chicago to effect open-housing laws. Here he encountered racial hatreds and fury even greater than those he had experienced in the South.

The slum neighborhood in which he took an apartment was an "island of poverty" within a city enjoying one of the highest per capita incomes in the world. From behind the ghetto walls, the blacks entrapped were well aware of the white suburbanites speeding, via elevated skyways and elaborate expressways, past the vast pockets of black deprivation. Allowed only the hardest, ugliest, and most menial jobs, they were just as aware that they were as capable as anyone else of building the tall towers of the modern city—but were excluded by white labor unions.

King wrote in his depressing apartment, looking out on streets where hundreds of children played, lacking playground facilities, and the phone rang daily with "countless stories of man's inhumanity to man." Constantly he found himself, he said, forced to struggle "against the depression and hopelessness which the hearts of our cities pump into the spiritual bloodstream of our lives." Of the children, King wrote:

> When you go out and talk to them you see the light of intelligence glowing in their beautiful dark eyes. Then you realize their overwhelming joy because someone has simply stopped to say hello; for they live in a world where even their parents are often forced to ignore them. In the tight squeeze of economic pressure, their mothers and fathers both must work; indeed, more often than not, the father will hold two jobs, one in the day and another at night. With the long distances ghetto parents must travel to work and the emotional exhaustion that comes from the daily struggle to survive in a hostile world, they are left with too little time or energy to attend to the emotional needs of their growing children.

Too soon you begin to see the effects of this emotional and environmental deprivation. The children's clothes are too skimpy to protect them from the Chicago wind, and a closer look reveals the mucus in the corners of their bright eyes, and you are reminded that vitamin pills and flu shots are luxuries which they can ill afford. The "runny noses" of ghetto children become a graphic symbol of medical neglect in a society which has mastered most of the diseases from which they will too soon die. There is something wrong in a society which allows this to happen.

King wrote *Chaos or Community?* to detail what was wrong; namely, that the most unconscionable horror of America's caves does not lie simply in the squalid housing, the woefully inadequate medical facilities (if any exist at all), the shockingly inferior educational facilities, the psychological violence of the environment promoting violent response among the caged, the lack of access to cultural institutions, or the absence of a "job network system" such as those that service communities outside.

No, the greatest horror lies in the fact that the purpose of the caves is to contain people within them: they are caverns of exclusion. No piecemeal and uncoordinated programs of education, welfare, jobs, or other aid will change the circumstances of the masses of people imprisoned within, King concluded. Rather, it is the very walls of the cave that must come tumbling down, and with them the notion of the acceptability of such implacable restraints on any people within society. Accordingly, the last crusade envisioned by King was a

Ossie, Ruby, and their children protest at a CORE (Congress of Racial Equality) peace demonstration, 1972. *(Bruce Davidson)*

Emceeing the March on Washington, August 1963.

Ossie with members of Actors' Equity en route to the Martin Luther King, Jr., Memorial March in Memphis, April 1968. *(Del Ankers Photographers)*

Ossie with John
Randolph (right)
and Frederick
Ewen, 1988.

At the March on City Hall, New York City,
1978. *(Amsterdam News File Photos)*

At the twentieth-anniversary celebration of the March on Washington, 1983.

Protesting the war in
Iraq, New York City,
2003. *(Hasna
Muhammad)*

At an anti-death-penalty rally, New York City,
c. 1994. *(Ihsaana Muhammad)*

At Howard University, Charter Day 2004. *(Ron Ceasar)*

At a radio interview, undated.

war by poor people and their allies against domestic poverty and a global campaign for the eradication of poverty, racism, and militarism.

Significantly, it was at this stage of the prophet's development that King was himself eliminated, the ruthless who engage in such tactics failing to recognize that a man's body may be eliminated but his spirit marches on.

Twenty-two years later, not only have the conditions within the caves worsened, but in the current tenacious hold of the old rationalizations, some African-Americans sense white endorsement—if not explicit, then by default—of black genocide.

For African-Americans in the current era, something irrevocably changes in the face of such a realization. There comes a time in history when the lessons are plain, when no excuse exists any longer for old partners to waltz in each other's arms—or at arm's length—in the same old dance of monstrous domination by the one and dehumanizing subjugation of the other. At that moment both partners are free to make choices, and those choices will determine the character of the new relationship.

King himself stands as a symbol of why the old order can never return. No more heroic, no more loving crusade to change the nation for the better has ever come about than the nonviolent crusade he led. Yet before he died, he was perfectly aware that the moral imperative so briefly honored would not be translated into committed political action by the federal government or by the people as a whole any more than had been true after the Revolutionary and the Civil Wars.

Before the end, he recognized that the struggle would have to be enlarged onto the world stage, and with uncanny foresight he laid out a new comprehensive strategy—and the choices—in *Chaos or Community?* On the eve of the twenty-first century, there seems to us little doubt that the most fundamental challenge facing the nation today is that of resurrecting the goal and pursuit of King's Poor People's Crusade and his quest for justice and peace worldwide.

Clearly, African-Americans must be in the vanguard in the building of such a movement. Not because we are inherently noble but because we have no choice if we are to save our children and thus have a future. To do this, those of us outside the caves must achieve solidarity with those within.

"Power, properly understood," King wrote, "is the ability to achieve purpose. It is the strength required to bring about social, political or economic changes. In this sense power is not only desirable but necessary in order to implement the demands of love and justice."

In whatever form power comes to the people, he indicates, it is most often by *organized* efforts to achieve it, essentially through three means: ideological, political, and economic.

Politically, we have recently witnessed a widening base of black voters and the successful implementation of alliances, as brilliantly pursued by Jesse Jackson and others on local and national levels, particularly in the South. Undoubtedly, that political base must specifically widen to catch the imagination and commitment of the masses of the ghetto disenfranchised and disillusioned. Currently, as men in Washington decree that tens of thousands of young black women will enter the cheap labor market through "workfare," it is interesting to contemplate the possibility of organizing teenage mothers into political units capable of exerting themselves to change their conditions on behalf of their children. Likewise, it is interesting to contemplate the possibility of organizing black male youth—currently under genocidal siege—on behalf of the same!

In the ideological arena, African-Americans occupy a position of uncommon and exciting advantage if we will only elevate our gaze high enough to recognize it. For, excluded from the ranks of the myth-makers in this land, we have historically had to deal with reality and with truth, in whatever form the truth came, if we were to survive and transcend. It is therefore we who are uniquely free to dream of a world without racism, poverty, war, sexism, and all the other "isms" that plague humankind. Given our present condition, we would be foolish indeed if we did not act on the dream!

Our advantage is that untold millions of people long for such a world. Ideologically, our philosophy is rooted in the simple humanism that has always been our strength: that however much it often seems to the contrary, most people wish to be better than they are, and they wish the world to be better. Through the ages, people have been capable of dying for such beliefs (African-Americans have contributed substantially to that roster); in the twenty-first century, perhaps millions will be willing to live for them. "Cooperation," then, rather than "competition" is the essential principle that we propose should govern human affairs. Is it not possible that through application of such a principle, humankind could effect a quantum leap in ethics sufficient to match the awesome (and frequently terrifying) technological advances?

On the world scene, one thing is clear. It is time that African-Americans do what Du Bois, Malcolm X, and King came to realize, each in his own time, had to be done: *elevate our struggle from the domestic arena of civil rights to the global level of human rights.* In doing so, we must bring history around full circle in reestablishing with the peoples of Africa the bonds of kinship severed so cruelly over four centuries. For the millions of black children occupying such terrible cages of war, poverty, and death in African lands are a phenomenon linked in history to the millions caged in America and other nations: the intolerable fruits of European plunder, colonialism, and neocolonialism extending into our times.

The most immediate responsibility faced by African-Americans is the restoration to black youth of their self-esteem and sense of place in a world so cruelly snatched from them every single day, and to encourage within them a visionary view.

A second great responsibility is that of teaching the nation, so that white Americans cannot continue to hide so grotesquely behind the myth of national equality while the relentless quiet and unquiet eradication of millions of their fellow citizens proceeds. The twentieth century has made such innocence obscene.

A century and a half ago, a free black from North Carolina living in Boston addressed an "Appeal . . . to the Colored Citizens of the World but in Particular and Very Expressly to Those of the United States of America." In four detailed parts, David Walker's appeal spelled out the crimes against African peoples, named the perpetrators, and called upon slaves to rise and cast off slavery, using whatever means they had to in order to end the monstrous system.

The document caused a sensation. The slave states unsuccessfully sought to suppress it, and Walker, in Boston, met a mysterious death. Walker's influence, however, as in the case of King, could not be curtailed. It was not William Lloyd Garrison's thunderous denunciation of slavery that initiated the organized abolitionist movement but Walker in his stirring call. At the close, Walker wrote that it seemed to him there had to be some purpose to all the suffering Africans had endured in their cruel transport from their homeland.

In the twentieth century, King must surely have agreed that at landmark stages in history, it is incumbent upon human beings to declare their purpose. Do not be afraid, he surely charges African-Americans in the spirit of one of the old black spirituals upon which he loved to draw, "Walk together, children. Don'cha get weary":

> In the days ahead we must not consider it unpatriotic to raise certain basic questions about our national character. We must begin to ask, "Why are there forty million poor people in a nation overflowing with such unbelievable affluence?" . . . Why have we substituted the arrogant undertaking of policing the whole world for the high task of putting our own house in order? . . . For its very survival's sake, America must reexamine old presuppositions and release itself from many things that for centuries have been held sacred. For the evils of racism, poverty, and militarism

to die, a new set of values must be born. Our economy must become more person-centered than property-and-profit centered. Our government must depend more on its moral power than on its military power.

Let us . . . be those creative dissenters who will call our . . . nation to a higher destiny, to a new plateau of compassion, to a more noble expression of humaneness.

We are superbly equipped to do this. We have been seared in the flames of suffering. We have learned from our have-not status that it profits a nation little to gain the whole world of means and lose the end, its own soul. We must have a passion for peace . . . Giving our ultimate allegiance to . . . justice . . . So in dealing with our particular dilemma, we will challenge the nation to deal with its larger dilemma.

This is the challenge. If we will dare to meet it honestly, historians in future years will have to say there lived a great people—a black people—who bore their burdens of oppression in the heat of many days and who, through tenacity and creative commitment, injected new meaning into the veins of American life.

If the challenge to African-Americans is to lead, the challenge to the nation is surely to follow. We have only to envision the prospect and undertake the task with the same determination and commitment of resources.

Let us, accordingly—all of us—get about the business of demolishing the walls of the caves!

# TRIBUTES
# AND
# EULOGIES

Tavis Smiley: *How does one prepare to eulogize one like Malcolm X . . . ?*

Ossie Davis: *The first thing, I should think, would be to sit quietly—for as long as it takes—and think long thoughts about the subject: about the time, about his life or her life, about where our people were in their march toward freedom and about where they are now. The great advantage of our having affairs like this is that it gives us a chance to revisit our heroes and to get our priorities back in order, so that as we move forward, we move with a sense of direction and purpose. So if someone asks you to eulogize an important figure, the first thing to do is to think, and then remember, and then speak.*

—On the *Tavis Smiley Show*, January 2005

# MALCOLM X

◆

*Faith Temple, Church of God, New York City*
*February 27, 1965*

R.D.: *Long accustomed to speaking extemporaneously, Ossie had planned to wait until the morning of the funeral to compose the eulogy. But the stiuation was so volatile, and there was so much to say—and it was so important that it be said—that I convinced him to get started the night before.*

O.D.: *Malcolm had been killed on Sunday afternoon. Tuesday night, Mosque 7—where Malcolm used to preach—was firebombed. Harlem seemed on the verge of open warfare. They thought a word from me might help to keep the peace.*

Here, at this final hour, in this quiet place, Harlem has come to bid farewell to one of its brightest hopes—extinguished now and gone from us forever.

For Harlem is where he worked and where he struggled and fought—his home of homes; where his heart was and where his people are—and it is, therefore, most fitting that we meet once again—in Harlem—to share these last moments with him.

For Harlem has been ever gracious to those who have loved her, have fought for her, and have defended her honor even to the death. It is not in the memory of man that this be-leaguered, unfortunate, but nonetheless proud community has found a braver, more gallant young champion than this Afro-American who lies before us—unconquered still.

I say the word again, as he would want me to: *Afro-American;* Afro-American Malcolm, who was a master, was most meticulous in his use of words. Nobody knew better than he the power words have over the minds of men. Malcolm had stopped being "Negro" years ago.

It had become too small, too puny, too weak a word for him. Malcolm was bigger than that. Malcolm had become an *Afro-American,* and he wanted—so desperately—that we, that all his people would become Afro-Americans too.

There are those who still consider it their duty, as friends of the Negro people, to tell us to revile him, to flee, even from the presence of his memory, to save ourselves by writing him out of the history of our turbulent times.

Many will ask what Harlem finds to honor in this stormy, controversial, and bold young captain. And we will smile.

Many will say turn away, away from this man, for he is not a man but a demon, a monster, a subverter, and an enemy of the black man. And we will smile.

They will say that he is of hate—a fanatic, a racist who can only bring evil to the cause for which you struggle.

And we will answer and say unto them: Did you ever talk to Brother Malcolm? Did you ever touch him, or have him smile at you? Did you ever really listen to him? Did he ever do a mean thing? Was he ever himself associated with violence or any public disturbance? For if you did, you would know him.

And if you knew him, you would know why we must honor him. Malcolm was our manhood, our living black manhood! This was his meaning to his people. And, in honoring him, we honor the best in ourselves.

Last year, from Africa, he wrote these words to a friend:

> My journey [he says] is almost ended, and I have a much broader scope than when I started out, which I believe will add new life and dimension to our struggle for freedom and honor, and dignity in the States. I'm writing these things so that you will know for a fact the tremendous sympathy and support we have among the African states for our Human-Rights Struggle. The main thing is that we keep a United Front wherein our most valuable time and energy will not be wasted fighting each other.

However much we may have differed with him—or with each other about him and his value as a man—let his going from us serve only to bring us together now. Consigning these mortal remains to earth, the common mother of all, secure in the knowledge that what we place in the ground is no more now a man, but a seed, which, after the winter of discontent, will come forth again to meet us. And we shall know him then for what he was and is—a Prince, our own black shining Prince, who didn't hesitate to die, because he loved us so.

# GODFREY CAMBRIDGE

The Washington Post, *December 5, 1976*

R.D.: *It's hard to write about Godfrey. If I hadn't been there, I wouldn't have believed. He was mythical and maddening: larger than life, something like John Henry or Paul Bunyan. Then sometimes he would seem to relate to Ossie like a baby brother seeking approbation.*

*That said, I don't recall the cab door actually coming off. As I remember it, the cab driver pulled away before Godfrey let go.*

Godfrey is gone, and in place of that black and wild barbaric yawp that was his personal response to living black in white America, there is now sorrow that is genuine and silence that is awkward, even embarrassing.

Godfrey was a cry of anguish, a scream at the top of the voice for help. We who knew him and loved him stood on the sidelines of his tragedy like tourists gawking at a cheap execution. We heard him, we heard him good: We knew where he was coming from, we knew why his life was on fire, but none of us ever found a way to come to his aid.

I invented a phrase which I hope will become a respectable cliché someday, which I have had occasion to use at several funerals, and which I suspect will still be appropriate when somebody will have cause to say a few brief last remarks over me: Every black man dies first of all from being black—the other cause of death is hardly worth putting down on the death certificate.

Even so, there is more than one way to die from being black: lead poisoning, dope addiction, being hungry too much, being stabbed to death by a brother on a street corner, high blood pressure, making the wrong white somebody mad at you, or throwing your life into the river or under the subway—and, there is Godfrey's way.

Now, it is true that Godfrey Cambridge was as hostile and violent as he was black. He had a temper that used to explode under him like a booster under a launching rocket. From time to time his temper drove him bad. Take that rainy night we were both in *Purlie Victorious* at the Longacre Theatre in New York. After the show, Godfrey hailed a cab, which slowed down until the driver saw that Godfrey was black. He speeded up, passing Godfrey by and splashing water on his clothes. But the light was red, the cab had to stop at the corner, where Ruby Dee, my wife, and I had been standing and watching. Ruby immediately stepped over to the cab, opened the door, and proceeded to give the driver a piece of her mind. (Ruby, like Godfrey, had been raised in the streets of Harlem and had learned well the art of screaming in self-defense. Me, I was born and raised in the South, and Mama had never encouraged me to express any opinion at variance with what a white man might be thinking— certainly not at the top of my voice.) The light changed, but not before Godfrey had run up to join Ruby at the door of the taxi and stood cursing the driver for being a racist bastard! The driver engaged his gear and speeded off, but not before Godfrey Cambridge with a sharp jerk of his bare hands had ripped the door completely off the hinges.

And then there was the time when Godfrey, not being able to open a locker door in his dressing room, took his fist and stove it in; or when conditions in his dressing room in spite of his continued complaints to the management had not been attended to, Godfrey took a fire axe and chopped the sink from the wall. He was frightening when the rage was upon him and undoubtedly, when provoked, the most violent man I ever met.

There was a time when I thought he had it beat. I had occasion to remark that success had come to Godfrey just in time to prevent him from killing somebody, but I was premature, Godfrey did kill somebody—he killed himself.

Godfrey did have success and for a while he had it all. America gave much to Godfrey, cars, houses, television specials, a big house in Connecticut, all the trappings of stardom, but what he needed most of all, it never gave and that was too much.

His sense of humor was genuine and productive. And in spite of his personal torment, Godfrey could laugh. Not only at the situation, but at himself. He was as black in outlook and attitude as any of the rest of us. And many a time, with a few friends gathered at his side, he would regale us with the latest chapter from his unending war against white bigots and black fools. And we laughed with Godfrey, couldn't help ourselves, laughing till we cried, partakers of shared memories of what it was like when we were all starving black actors waiting for the world to notice, and how the more things changed, the more they remained the same.

It was at these times when Godfrey was at his golden best—all of us together swimming in that rich communion so dear and necessary to blacks. This sense of belonging to ourselves and to each other in a way that guaranteed our own black self-esteem. Our way of looking at ourselves in spite of the big white world out there and being deeply satisfied with what we saw. And sometimes this common bond, this shared self-evaluation is all we need to heal us from the hurts.

For some of us, this meeting of friendly eyes, this pressing of hands, this wallowing in the warmth of one another is all we need to cope, to continue, to keep going. But for Godfrey, no. He needed something else. He needed more than white America's recognition. He needed more than appreciation. He needed more than stardom. He needed love. Godfrey needed love and that's what killed him. For the bond of common affairs in our country is not love but hypocrisy. And hypocrisy when it sits smiling on the face of a bigot was too much for Godfrey to bear.

Godfrey needed love and he needed it from the whites. But America was not ready to love Godfrey. It was prepared to kiss him on both cheeks, but not on the lips. Not yet. Godfrey died of unrequited love. In his frustrated, unappeased, unvented rage, he had to destroy something and in the end, it was himself he killed, his heart breaking under the overload of unexpressed hostility.

He killed himself and that was too much of a price to pay.

But he gave as good as he got. And many an ex-bigot owes his current enlightenment in matters of race relations to the fact that Godfrey Cambridge was always ready to put his foot squarely up some arrogant bigot's behind. And many times, as the rest of us stood on the sidelines watching, he did just that.

Right on, brother. Sleep well.

# LOUIS ARMSTRONG

### 1980

R. D.: *Ossie wrote and performed this tribute to Louis Armstrong (as well as the following one to Stepin Fetchit) during our public television series,* With Ossie & Ruby.

L ouis Armstrong was a dangerous man, too, but it took me a long time to find that out. Most of the fellows I grew up with, myself included, we used to laugh at Louis Armstrong. We knew he was good, but that didn't save him from our malice and our ridicule. Everywhere we'd look, there'd be Louis—sweat popping, eyes bugging, mouth wide open, grinning, oh my Lord, from ear to ear. *Ooftah,* we called him—mopping his brow, ducking his head, doing his thing for the white man. "Oh yeahhhh . . . !"

It was not till 1966, when we were working on a picture together in New York with Sammy Davis, Jr., and Cicely Tyson, that I got to know Louis better. Everybody on the set thought it was a ball. Louis and Sammy . . . they never stopped lying, jiving, putting each other down for the benefit of the crowds. It was happy times with two master clowns in charge, keeping the whole set in stitches.

One day, we had broken for lunch, and I had decided to stay in. It was quiet, and I thought everybody else had gone out. I started back towards the set to lie down, and there near the doorway was Louis, sitting in a chair staring up and off into space, with the saddest, most heartbreaking expression I'd ever seen on a man's face. And for a moment, I just stood and stared. I tried to turn and sneak away, but the noise I made snapped Louis out of it and all at once his face broke into that big professional smile, his mouth open. And he whipped out his handkerchief, mopped his brow, and growled, "Look out dere, Pops, you cats must be trying to starve ol' Louis to death, yeah . . ."

I put on my face and grinned right back. But it wasn't funny. Not anymore. What I saw in that look shook me: it was my father, my uncle, myself, down through the generations doing exactly what Louis had had to do, and for the same reason—to survive.

I never laughed at Louis after that. Beneath that gravel voice and that shuffle, under all that mouth, wide as a satchel with more grinning teeth than a piano got keys, was a horn that could kill a man. That horn was where Louis kept his manhood hid all those years . . . enough for him . . . enough for all of us.

Louis, man, I didn't have sense enough to tell you this when I was a kid—I didn't even know it myself—but I love you. And I ain't the only one.

# STEPIN FETCHIT

## 1981

Another movie stereotype that knew exactly what he was doing was Stepin Fetchit. Dumb, ignorant, head-scratching—oh, he was one of America's favorites. The man who created Stepin Fetchit, Lincoln Perry, he made Hollywood comfortable and Hollywood made him rich. There he was in the bottom of the Depression, driving around in a chauffeur-driven Rolls-Royce limousine. Man, oh man. The whole country laughed when old Step's pictures came to town, especially the good white citizens of Waycross, Georgia, where I grew up as a boy. There they'd be, downstairs at the Saturday night movie looking up at that dumb stupid darkey up on the silver screen and laughing to split their sides. And me and my buddies, we'd be up in the balcony where all the black folks had to sit according to the law, and we'd be laughing just as loud as they did, but we weren't laughing at Stepin Fetchit; we were laughing at them.

Now, the good black citizens of Waycross, Georgia, did not like Stepin Fetchit one bit, nor the influence they thought he had on us. They thought that his shuffling, shiftless, Dumb Darkey routine made us all look inferior to the white folks, and they hated him for that. And they tried to warn us away from the theatre. They were embarrassed by all that stuff that Step was doing. But we weren't embarrassed. We didn't think that Stepin Fetchit was dumb; we thought he was smart—smart enough to pull the wool over the eyes of the white folks and make them like it. Running a game on the boss man—a dangerous game, but winning all the way. Old Step, he made us believe that even in the bottom of slavery black folks must have had some victories.

Consider a slave like old Stepin Fetchit: so dumb that if the master sent him to get a hoe, he would come back with a plow; if he told him to go and kill a chicken, he would go out and kill a cow; or if he said go to the fields and go to work, Old Step would misunderstand and go back to his shack and sit down. And then when the old master would get so mad and furious that he'd run after Step with a whip raised on high, Step would just stand there, not understanding what was going on, scratching his head and grinning. Finally he would probably just sit down under a tree and go to sleep. Oh, ho! Such a man would have been a total disaster in the cotton patch. So, just think of what would have happened if all the slaves had been smart enough to be as dumb as old Stepin Fetchit. Why, nothing at all would have happened on the plantation; slavery would have had to go out of business in a couple of weeks. Well, that's what we thought.

And anyway, nobody ever got lynched when Stepin Fetchit pictures were in town. He made everybody feel so comfortable and so superior that they didn't need to go out and hurt anybody. No, they would just sit there in their seats, look up at that screen and laugh and laugh at our hero: a one-man strike against that system, but they didn't know it. Old Stepin Fetchit—the man who invented the coffee break in the cotton patch.

# THE SCHOMBURG CENTER

### Fundraiser, Date Unknown

R.D.: *When I was growing up, it was the 135th Street Library, home of the Arthur A. Schomburg Collection of Negro Literature and Art. I would go there with my sisters and brother; it was one of the few places Mother would let us go on our own. I won my first prize there—a box of jelly beans for a poem I'd written. Later, it was home to the American Negro Theatre, where I began my life as an actor. Over the years, the library expanded, eventually becoming the Schomburg Center for Research in Black Culture. Ossie and I were pleased to lend our support to this place, which had nurtured us for so long in so many ways. And still does.*

When I arrived poor and penniless, an immigrant from the land of Waycross, Georgia, the Negro Question then agitating the entire country could be phrased as succinctly then as it is now: When do we eat?

Landing at Pennsylvania Station—the black man's Ellis Island—with $30, the problem of where to stay, what to wear—if anything—and how to eat, especially after that thirty was gone, was excruciatingly urgent and immediate.

There was only one sure place a lost and lonely boy like me could turn in my desperate hour of need: the library—and of course, the Schomburg Collection, as it was then called.

Now, I have always been more interested in collard greens

than culture, so why did my flight from imminent starvation lead me here? Thereby hangs a tale: I was hungry, but in spite of the fact that it was still the Great Depression, I had been to the movies. I had seen how Jimmy Cagney, George Raft, Edward G. Robinson, and Humphrey Bogart had solved the nutritional deficit with which they were afflicted: they went to the bank, they passed a note to the teller, saying "Give me your money," the tellers responded with alacrity—and also, more importantly, with whatever cash they had. Ladies and Gentlemen, I am not ashamed to confess that in my hour of need, I too, resorted to highway robbery, but not with a pistol. I did it with a poem. And the result was exactly the same.

By way of further background, let me say that in those good old golden days of the Great Depression, Harlem was heaven. And, in the instance of Father Divine, Harlem was more than one heaven—they were dotted all over the place, just as the libraries were, and every one of those heavens had a dining room where a person could go in, sit down, and order a full-course meal, eat to his heart's content—and all for fifteen cents. All I needed to make my daily dietary ends meet was fifteen cents.

So, every day I would go to the library and pass my hold-up note to the teller—who in institutions like these is called a *librarian*—a note that would go somewhat like this, quoting from memory:

> My very dear Librarian:
>
> The bulge you see in my pocket is a poem. One false move and I will jump up on a table in the reading room and recite it all over the place.

I could see the astonishment and fear in their eyes, as they tried hard to keep from laughing. Then they read the rest of the note:

I greet you from starvation—all I need
Is 15 cents, so I can go and feed.
This poem is thus for sale, for rent or barter,
I'll even make it two poems for a quarter.

But if you dally, I will drop down dead,
A poet's hungry blood be on your head!
Donate at once . . . set my poor stomach free.
Signed: Georgia Boy, whose other name is Me.

And, thanks to all those poetry-loving librarians who invested—sometimes 15 cents, sometimes a quarter—not only did I refuse to starve myself to death, I am still here. And if poetry could outwit poverty 48 years ago, I have no doubt that it can do so now! Schomburg Center for Research in Black Culture needs $14,570,000 in the same desperate sense I needed to get over to Father Divine's before the kitchen closed. And I am prepared to be as shameless in hustling for my cultural hunger now as I was for my umbilical hunger then! I mean, I have got iambic pentameter I ain't used yet—and every one of them loaded! Any individual, institution, or corporation wanting to buy a couple of bushels for the cause—slightly warmed-over but made to order! We'll even give you a rebate— just give your names to the Secretary!

Thank you.

# BETTY SHABAZZ

～

*Riverside Church, 1997*

R.D.: *We decided to make our remembrance of Betty Shabazz a family affair. Ossie and I, who had known Malcolm, Betty, and their daughters for so many years, folded our words together like arms around the family—an image so eloquently evoked by the poetry of our daughter, Hasna.*

OSSIE:

Yesterday was Harlem's day of Lamentation
Great was our grief, and great our cause for
Grieving. Just as Ezekiel said:

Our bones were dry, our hopes were lost, we
Were cut off from our parts, for
Betty Shabazz—Malcolm's Beloved, who when she
Heard the shot that tore his heart out,
Spread wide her arms and
Covered her brood like an eagle!
Then stood her guard where Malcolm lies forever.
Red fires of outrage burning in her posture
"You shall not kill my man a second time!"—
That Betty . . . That Betty Shabazz—was dead!

That violence which 10,000 days ago took
Malcolm—from which we have yet to recover—
Came back to claim his Betty—two devastations
In a single blow. But that was yesterday.

Yesterday, Death claimed his right to push his mean agenda—
Trampled our hope, filled another grave
And slammed the door of suffering in our face.
Claiming as his the prize that had no price,
And left us emptied out—

But that was yesterday.

Today, Betty has passed over, and so have we.
From Lamentation into Hallelujah.
Harlem is no stranger to grief: we've been to
Hell before, and back again.
Death will not—cannot—
Have the final word. We have been black too
Long to grant him that. That honor goes to
Betty. Not to Death!

And there are questions here, Death cannot answer:
We ask you, Death, must partings be forever?
Are there no bonds that stretch beyond the grave?
Can we not hope that somewhere just beyond the
Veil of yesterday, in a world composed of
Children, Betty still stands, waiting to hear
From us.
And this we say to her now:
Betty . . . God keep you safe and warm and close

To Malcolm
Surely, from all this blood and fire, some
Solace, in your name, will take the air.
From all this death your face will rise again,
Singing Percy Bysshe Shelley's song of hope:
"And we will hope till hope itself creates
From its own wreck the thing it contemplates."
And are we not from your experiences and with
Your help, the children of Hope?

Death may take only what is his by Nature's Law,
The rest belongs to us, the rest is ours.
Go well, Sister Betty:
Your journey ends, and Malcolm—
Steps from the shadows to greet his much Beloved
Fresh from yesterday's deep and pain-filled river,
And Malcolm will embrace you, and kiss you,
And whisper in your ear, Well done, Betty.
May Allah, The Merciful, grant you mercy.
May God, who loves all children, grant you peace.

To the family, to all who here assemble, to
All the world:
Grieve if you must, but children are still dying.
Grieve, but be brief.
There's fighting to be done.

RUBY:

Though many of us came to know Betty
Shabazz as the wife of Malcolm X—

Our Warrior Prince—on the day of
His Murder, she moved from the
Shadows as the guardian of his
Legacy and gradually, into a legacy of her own.
Throwing herself into the struggle
To deflect the bullets ricocheting
Through the centuries. She became a
Warrior in her own right—Touching
Lives as Teacher, Administrator,
Agitator, Citizen. And it is to
This Betty, this Sister, this
Mother, this Woman, this Friend—
That we speak today:

We didn't want to let you go.
They said there was a 10-to-20% Chance
You could survive. It was slim.
But knowing you, Betty,
Your fierce determination to overcome,
To raise your children,
To graduate—Dr. Shabazz,
To see that whatever you attended be well done,
If anybody could, we knew you'd work that
Miracle and live.
We were not prepared.
We didn't want to let you go.
Surely, our prayers would help see
You through.
Surely your strength would do all the rest—
And you would move among us again,

Comfort us against murder and madness.
You were so much woven into the fabric of our
Hope, no matter the warnings.
We were not prepared.
We did not want to let you go.

What now is your agenda?
What is it your death is trying to make us see
About our times,
Our minds,
Our work,
Our love,
And above all else—our Children?
How can we save them from confusion,
Warn them against the coming of the Thingdom
Of greed and grossness?
How can we seed the clouds of our times with
Greater Compassion
And Wisdom
And Love
So that the waters of the coming storms
Will cleanse us,
And we can bathe the babies in virtue
And in joy?
We did not want to let you go,
But Allah called your name
And you have stepped out of the Marching Line
Making us pay attention
Making us see ourselves
Turning our heads towards

Righteousness and peace.
And so we must leave you now, dear Sister Betty
Beside the still waters and the green pastures,
Scouting the Heavens for
More light to see us through.


## DEAR SISTERS*
*(Attallah, Qubilah, Ilyasah, Gamilah, Malikah, and Malaak)*

My mothers and fathers
and sisters and brothers
and cousins and children
will be for you
We will encircle you
and protect you,
as you pull your Selves together

Our arms
are wrapped around
your arms
Your arms
around his young, tender arms
and we will never let go

We will hold you
and rock you
and hum your mother and father's song
Not in their place

---

Not in their voice
but in our way

As you need us
As you heal through this
and any other
reality
we are stretched firm and wide
around you
We will pray and be for you
We are your parents now

——HASNA MUHAMMAD

# A TRIBUTE TO HEROES:
# THEN AND NOW

~

*National Press Club*
*May 2002*

R.D.: *Some of Ossie's friends and acquaintances on the Left expressed surprise and dismay at his yearly participation in the National Memorial Day Concert in Washington, D.C. To one such letter of protest, Ossie replied: "I believe, with W.E.B. Du Bois, that all wars—even those fought in good causes—are evil. But some—such as the American Revolutionary War, the Civil War—are wars that had to be fought . . . I volunteered to join the fight against Hitler, and would do so again. I think there were many thousands of brave men and women who thought, felt, and acted as I did, some of whom gave their lives. I believe that these men and women deserve to be remembered. And that's why, this coming May, I have agreed to serve again as Master of Ceremonies. In their name and for their honor."*

On May 5, 1868, General John A. Logan of the Army of the Republic, an organization of former sailors and soldiers, issued the following proclamation:

> The 30th of May is designated for the purpose of strewing with flowers, or otherwise decorating the graves of comrades who died in defense of their country during the late

rebellion, and whose bodies now lie in almost every city, village, and hamlet churchyard in the land. In this observance no form of ceremony is prescribed, but posts and comrades will in their own way arrange such fitting services and testimonials of respect as circumstances may permit.

This 1868 celebration was inspired by local observances of the day in several towns throughout America that had taken place in the three years since the Civil War. Several Northern and Southern cities claim to be the birthplace of Memorial Day, including Columbus, Mississippi, Macon, Georgia, Richmond, Virginia, Boalsburg, Pennsylvania, and Carbondale, Illinois. In 1966, the federal government, under the direction of President Lyndon Johnson, made Waterloo, New York, the official birthplace of Memorial Day, because Waterloo, ever since its first celebration in 1866, had made Memorial Day an annual event, during which businesses were closed and residents decorated the graves of soldiers and sailors with flowers and flags.

During World War I, the honor was extended to include not just those who fell in the Civil War, but also to those who had died in all of America's wars. In 1971 Congress declared Memorial Day a national holiday, to be celebrated the last Monday in May.

We already see, in this small capsule of history, how a simple act of sorrow, grief, and remembrance, passed year after year from one cemetery to another, one city, one state, to another until, finally, the entire nation had embraced it. Memorial Day now speaks to all Americans, from all Americans. It is officially celebrated at Arlington National Cemetery, with a ceremony in which an American flag is placed on every grave. It is also customary for the president or the vice president to give a speech honoring the priceless contributions of the dead and lay a wreath at the Tomb of the Unknown Soldier.

But there are some who've always wanted Memorial Day to be more. An occasion of wider public observance seems in order, where not only the military, but also the rest of the nation could join in this solemn yet uplifting tribute and remembrance. And so, every year, rain or shine, since 1990 some of us have gathered on the West Lawn of the Capitol to express our feelings by giving a concert, a concert to which the entire nation is—both physically and electronically—invited to attend. And it is this concert, and why we feel it important, that brings me before you today to tell our story.

First, we are much aware of how important these national public occasions can be. How they serve the function of bringing us Americans together to periodically renew our bonds with the country we call our home; a chance to refurbish our commitment, to reactivate—by rituals and national amenities—the civic sinews that declare to all the world that we are One People. Despite our differences in histories and language, as black, white, Jew, Gentile, Catholic, Protestant, and Muslim, Asian, Hispanic, and Native American—One People: E Pluribus Unum. A day for us all to stand in one accord.

A theme this mighty calls for appropriate display and pageantry. So we say let the music swell, the trumpets sing, the drums show forth their thunder, the national banners float in the ambient air. And bring the children, too, and let them see—by the gleam they see in your eyes, by the things the national anthem can do to stiffen your spine—what it means to be an American. Do not be afraid to become emotional over all the things about America that make you proud . . . or make you ashamed. Tell them about Crispus Attucks, the very first man to die in the American Revolution, and he was black, and also of the five thousand blacks who fought in that war before the United States was even born—our vote of confidence. Tell them of Gettysburg, where brave men on both sides gave their blood to decide the basic meaning of this land we love.

But days like these can serve a private purpose, certainly for me. A chance to call the roll, to summon up from the deep halls of Memory my own company roster of heroes past and present—some still alive, some dead in far-off places. A citizen-soldier I, taking inventory, voting this year's behavior up or down, catechizing my losses and my gains, confronting my doubts, confirming my affirmations, rendering final judgments on outcomes still undecided. What should this Memorial Day mean to all my comrades, to their wives, their families, to ones they left behind? What does the Memorial signify to *me*? The following poem, "In Flanders Fields," by John McCrae, is another way for me to put the question:

IN FLANDERS FIELDS

In Flanders fields the poppies blow
Between the crosses, row on row,
That mark our place; and in the sky,
The larks, still bravely singing, fly
Scarce heard amid the guns below.

We are the Dead. Short days ago
We lived, felt dawn, saw sunset glow,
Loved and were loved, and now we lie
In Flanders fields.

Take up our quarrel with the foe:
To you from falling hands we throw
The torch; be yours to hold it high.
If ye break faith with us who die
We shall not sleep, though poppies grow
In Flanders fields.

I had an uncle Rafe, my father's youngest brother, who fought in World War I and died in France the year that I was born. He lies among his peers, perhaps in Flanders fields. My pledge to him is based on more than blood, for I was a soldier, too, in World War II. Some part of me still is, and will always be, until the day I die. I see them clearly, even now, the men in my old outfit as they report for duty in my mind . . . what they meant to me, and I to them. We were the 25th Station Hospital, the first such outfit ever to be authorized by the army with all African-American personnel, except for the two white medical officers at the top.

The first great deployment of American military might was already on its way to meet Erwin Rommel and his panzer divisions in North Africa. The campaign was expected to be long and fierce and bloody. Our job at the 25th Station was to receive the wounded flown down to us from the battlefield, stabilize them, then put them in planes for the long flight back to America.

We at the 25th were the best, and we knew it; a very special group of men, chosen from the ranks of the Medical Corps, and sent to the Army Medical Center at Walter Reed Hospital, here in Washington, where we had been trained . . . and trained . . . and trained again. Oh yes, we were the best and we knew it. And then they sent us off to Liberia, West Africa. Black men, black officers—except the two at the top. And there we waited.

I remember with still-swelling pride what special people we were, and the bond—unverbalized, but not untested—that held us together; what a mighty oath we swore to one another, but never said a word. Our language was, instead, a certain look in the eye, a touch, an elevated shoulder, a shared sense of strength in every handshake. Faith to the death in each other, and also in the cause for which we were prepared to die.

I remember the letters from home, passing around the pictures of our wives and of our girlfriends, the raucous lies, the bravado, the tall tales that kept us laughing. Something developing among us, deeper than brother's blood, and growing deeper. Boasting, bragging loud enough for even Death to hear. Though segregated, were we not still Americans? What if we had to fight American racism with one hand, and German fascism with the other—what else was new? Were we not still Americans? Death, and the fear of Death, was cast from among us. We built an impregnable edifice in our minds, our hearts, and our imaginations: our own version of America— by our own hands, our own brand of patriotism, with a duty to each other and to all our people—high as, if not higher than, our duty to our country; a black man's justification for fighting a white man's war.

Nobody wrote it down, it was never codified; we never signed any papers, or raised our right hands, or repeated it for the record. But it was there, as palpable as the cables made of steel. It holds me hostage to it to this very day.

But in our deep and personal times and spaces, when quiet prevailed and everything was dark, and pride of race, and shame of segregation and the shabby way the Army treated us—all that and the rest of the world is put aside, and every man is trapped within himself, we dreamed the dream that every soldier dreams. And prayed the selfsame prayer: Lord, this life of mine may not mean much to others, but it's all I got. I'm willing to die if I have to, for Mama, my loved ones, my people, and even for my country; but don't let it be for nothing. You've seen me, Lord, sitting among my comrades when talking time was over . . . sharing what none of us would dare to put into words. Thinking faraway and sometimes dangerous thoughts as we wrestled with our duty, trying to give shape and meaning to what we knew was madness and despair . . . to find the urgent need to kill somebody. Somebody you didn't even know, who didn't know you. Searching, searching . . . each night, when taps have been sounded, and the blackout has been called, still looking for what's not written on the barrack walls. Searching somewhere out there in the darkness, across some far horizon, looking for the friendly face atop some future sunrise that was finally coming to meet us—looking for Peace.

I never met a soldier, Lord, who didn't want it—Peace—

and want it bad . . . who—sick to death of the endless nights and days of blood and pain, the hunger, the agony, the stench, the smoke, the bickering, of gunfire all night long—who hadn't prayed in the deepest part of his secret heart this ancient soldier's prayer: *Lord, if I could just know, that with my death that war would be over forever . . . that humankind had finally found a way to stop killing each other. Then, no matter how I died, or when, or where, I could accept it, Lord, and then I could sleep in peace.*

Many things have changed since World War II. America has changed, and so have we, within the military and without, not only for black folk, but also for other ethnic groups, and certainly for women. Much of what we fought for, and died for, inside our country and outside, has come to pass. And that is all to the good.

Still . . .

A year or so before he died, my wife and I were with Jackie Robinson at a prayer breakfast in Chicago. We felt his heartbreak as he stood before a crowded auditorium of mostly black people and said how he still found it impossible to salute the American flag—a flag under which he had fought as a soldier—and to recite the Pledge of Allegiance. We don't know to what degree, or whether ever, Jackie Robinson and the country he loved became reconciled. Even at the end, racism still tied his tongue.

Jackie's not the only one who has to temper his own patriotism with some reservations. There is a song we'll probably be singing come Sunday, which states flat out "This Is God's Country," as if it were God instead of us who took it away from the Native Americans. I have no intention of ever singing that particular song. I do not feel my patriotism is in the least impugned by that omission.

But...

Too much of the blood that puts the red into the Star-Spangled Banner is blood that came from black veins. I *know* what I'm saluting when that vaunted banner floats in my direction, and I know why I stand up straight, and give it the best that I've got. I do it for my grandchildren, for Uncle Rafe. I do it for all comrades in the 25th Station Hospital, dead or alive. To honor the America we dreamed of, those many nights in the barracks, swatting mosquitoes. The America we swore we would help to build, even if it cost us our lives.

This is, indeed, Memorial Day; fitting and proper it is that we should pay tribute, should make parade, should stand in solemn salute, should sing and dance and concertize in honor of those who died, heroes then, and heroes now—from Crispus Attucks, first to die on the Boston Common, March 5, 1770, down to the last brave man or woman who died but yesterday in far-off Afghanistan.

Sometimes this country did break faith. We have not paid in full the enormous debt we owe to all our heroes. To Abraham Lincoln—and was he not a patriot and a hero?—who asked of us before he died, that we should "bind up the nation's wounds, to care for him who shall have borne the battle, and for his widow, and his orphan—to do all which may achieve and cherish a lasting peace among ourselves and with all nations." To Martin Luther King—and was he not a patriot and a hero?—who warned us against the folly of violence as a solution to our problems, who said to us that we must finally "learn to live together as brothers, or perish together as fools"; whose example still teaches me that any war against terrorism that is not also a full-out war against racism, poverty, disease, the degradation of women and children, and despair, is a war that cannot be won!

No . . .

We citizens, and lovers and beneficiaries of America's bounty, profiting as we have from her commitment to democracy and freedom, have not kept our commitment to the fallen and finally built the city that shines on a hill. So that all who died believing in the promise of America, and in her total commitment to freedom and democracy, who lie at home or in some far-off Flanders field, shall not have died in vain. We have not, in my opinion, kept absolute faith with those who lie in Flanders fields.

Not yet.

But it's not too late.

Is that not one of the lessons of 9/11? Did not we Americans immediately drop all the things that made us different, and turn without a second thought, and face the challenge? Was there not, in what we saw and did, a patriotism that doesn't have to pick up a gun or wear a soldier's uniform to be a hero? The many firemen, and the policemen (several of whom were black) who died in the line of duty, numbering more than the number who died at Concord . . . were they not heroes in every honorable sense of the word—heroes and martyrs, too?

No, it is never too late for true and honest patriotism, no

matter what its form. But now and then we need to be reminded. So let me close with an invitation, which is also a challenge. Join us on Sunday night, May 26, on the West Lawn of the Capitol. Respond anew to the Flanders Fields Imperative. America is still the Land Where It's Never Too Late. Never, ever, too late for us to begin again. In tribute to all our heroes, then and now.

I thank you.

# JOHN RANDOLPH

~

*June 2004*


R.D.: *It seems like we knew John all our lives—he and his wife, Sarah Cunningham, were some of the best friends we had. Our kids often slept in the same bed while we stayed up all night strategizing in the daring dangerous days of McCarthy. They were, to quote from my poem about them:*

> Two sheltering rocks against the wind forever
> To whom the least could always turn, and turn again.
> Two lights in a large and single welcome window . . .


One of the things I used to look forward to, in those mad days when great issues were being debated on the floors of Actors' Equity, was that point in the meeting when John Ephrat would take the stage and read the names of the dearly departed. How I longed for John to read my name!

John Randolph meant so much to so many—each of us, I'm sure, has stories that we could tell illustrating the wonderful qualities of this human being. But I want to tell you about John before I knew John. I came into the theatre in '46 and '47, along with African-Americans who had just been invited down from Harlem to Broadway. I had met Ruby

Dee in a Broadway play called *Jeb.* We were subsequently hired to be in *Anna Lucasta,* which was on Broadway. And at that time, I was introduced to the Union and the magic of the microphone—and sometimes, the excitement of rising to a point of order, "Mr. Chairman . . . !"—and forgetting what you had to say. But what a magnificent way to audition, with all those actors watching you.

Here we came, from Harlem and various other places. What kind of reception did we get on Broadway? The most welcoming, the most gentle, the most inspiring, and the most active. Because when we got onto Broadway, there were people doing things that made us feel not only at home as actors, but put us in the middle of the struggle, which was helping to define us and our place in the world at that time. Remember, World War II was about racism, and America at the end of the war seemed for a moment to be determined that it should never happen again.

And the place where that passion was expressed most vividly in my mind was the theatre. And so, when we came to the places where we were met as actors onstage, there were always people who came around with little slips saying, "Tonight after the show, we're going to go to So-and-So's house down in the Village. We're gonna raise funds for Willie McGee in Mississippi." Or, "We're gonna raise funds for Rosa Lee Ingram in Florida. Her boys are in jail because they defended her honor." Or, "Down in Monroe, Georgia, four black people— two soldiers and their wives—were killed by the Ku Klux Klan, and we're gonna raise funds." And every night, something good would be happening. And we would go to these parties. And in one corner would be Paul Robeson; in another one would be Orson Welles—with Marlon Brando coming in the door.

Now, somebody got these parties together. Somebody passed out the invitations. Somebody told us how to get there. And that's how I first became acquainted with John Randolph, the Great Facilitator. I always found myself at the right place at the right time because somehow, John was involved— John, Bill Ross, and others—and they showed me the mechanics of how to be effective as an Equity member. So when great issues came to the floor, I was already coached—we'd had pre-meetings, and made determinations as to who was going to say what on what great issue, such as whether or not we wanted our country to share the knowledge of the atom bomb with the Russians. We actors took ourselves and our responsibility in fashioning the postwar world quite seriously.

And in these heady years—1947, when India was free, and Jackie Robinson was knocking it out of the park, and all of these things had significance—there was this community to which I belonged called Broadway, and it was inhabited by these marvelous, wonderful, creative people who made me feel more than welcome, who helped me define myself and my responsibilities as a human being when I came back from the war. And who, when the blacklist came, and when the powers that be decided to shut that raucous bunch of troublemakers on Broadway down by initiating these witch hunts, these were the people who helped structure a response that made sense, who helped organize a way to fight back.

Now, I had seen Hollywood respond when the powers

that be in Washington decided to get serious about making actors shut their mouths. I'd seen Hollywood close up, shut down, and great people who were out there decide to come back to Broadway, where they found that the response to governmental intrusion was quite different. Broadway stood up; Equity stood up. And that was not accidental. People were involved. John was involved. John Randolph, walking up and down Broadway with a suit that had many pockets. And each pocket was a cause. And if you met John, you wound up contributing to many of his pockets.

Ruby and I got to know John better when we were part of *The World of Sholom Aleichem.* And there we met Sarah, and we soon found ourselves—John, Ruby, Sarah, and me—as a little group of traveling troubadours. Whatever the cause was—if it was a strike, if it was a demonstration, if it was a rally—we four would show up and read some appropriate literature that stimulated response to the cause.

I remember on one occasion, it had been decided that we were going to pay a tribute to A. Philip Randolph. I got all the material and wrote a little sketch for four voices—radio theatre, or whatever we called it in those days—about fifteen to twenty minutes. It was going to be on Sunday; so on Sunday we came down to Carnegie Hall and rehearsed it. A. Philip was there and saw the rehearsal. We were prepared that night to pay this wonderful tribute, but we found out that his wife was not going to be able to come because she was paralyzed, confined to a wheelchair up in Harlem.

So John had this magnificent idea: since she cannot come to our performance, why not get in a cab, take the performance to her? Which is exactly what we did. We got in the cab, took our scripts, went up to the Dunbar Apartments in Harlem, went into the living room, where A. Philip Randolph and his wife—Bunny, I think he called her—sat on the couch and we performed. Oh, we laid it on heavy! She was crying with the passion that we gave to that performance.

To me, John was the essence of the beauty of the commitment to the struggle. John had a lifestyle that made all of the awful things we encountered somehow beautiful and glowing and glistening. And if you participated on his level, you could share the joy he always seemed to feel in the Struggle. I never met John where he didn't laugh or have some joy in contemplating the battle he was about to go into. I was worried, a lot of other people were worried, too; but John always was singing the victory song even before the battle was fought. That was a part of the joy he shared with us.

So, John, now that you're up there—if you do see John Ephrat, tell him how to say my name, will you?

# JAMES BOGGS

◄▬►

*Detroit, Michigan*
*October 23, 1993*

R.D.: *Ossie and I first encountered James Boggs in 1963 through his book* The American Revolution. *Jimmy was a laborer and an auto worker with no college education (yet seemingly born with a Ph.D.), but his book struck us as a prophecy, a voice crying out from the roots of the country. We bought up copies to send to everyone we knew. Over the years, we grew close to Jimmy and his wife, Grace Lee Boggs; and their lifelong commitment to community-based activism continued to inspire our own thinking.*

It has been our lot, Ruby's and mine, to run into and out of Grace and Jimmy's life, somewhat as we are doing this afternoon. Hit-and-run revolutionists, I guess you could call us. Always on the move, but blessed by having had some moments that we could come and spend with Jim and Grace.

I am, to some degree, a product of the Baptist church. All of my grandfathers were ministers, all my uncles, all the men in my family except my father—he was an honest man.

One of the biblical passages I always loved was Christ's response to Nicodemus: "You must be born again"—not going back to the womb, of course, but undergoing some fundamental change if you are going to save your life. There were several moments when, because of Jimmy, I was indeed born again.

I remember the appearance, under the aegis of *Monthly Review*, of a little book, *The American Revolution: Pages from a Negro Worker's Notebook*. This little book came into my life, I read every word of it, and it opened my mind. When I read it, I said, "Yes, of course. Amen. Even I could have thought of that." Immensities of thought reduced to images so simple that coming away from the book I was indeed born again. I could see the Struggle in a new light. I was recharged; my batteries were full; and I was able to go back to the Struggle carrying this book as my banner. Ruby and I bought up copies and mailed them to all the civil rights leaders—Martin Luther King Jr., Malcolm X, Whitney Young. We thought all of them should have an opportunity to be born again.

I remember when Jimmy was at Columbia University talking about our love of Africa. The movement for freedom on the African continent had had a tremendously inspiring effect on the Struggle over here. Some of us were so moved that we changed our hairstyles; we had our dashikis. And some of us thought that everything had been golden and marvelous and beautiful until the time they had taken us from Africa and brought us over here. James was talking about Africa and the culture, and he mentioned the leadership and some of the great kings of Africa. And he wound up saying, "Whatever you say, a king is a son-of-a-bitch even if he is an African king." All of a sudden my mind opened up, lightning struck. I was born again. I saw the dashiki and the hairdo in an entirely different light.

At that time, in addition to romanticizing Africa, we thought of land as a source not only of power and wealth but of identity. We thought we had to own some land in this country, that the government should cede black folks some land on which we could build our factories, and establish our communities, and let the rest of the world go hang. Then I came across this article by Jimmy in *The Liberator*. The title simply said, "The City Is the Black Man's Land." The bells rang, the lights went on, and I was born again. I was disenchanted with my romantic concept that we had to go out and establish our flag on some of God's territory and let the rest of the world go hang. Rather, we had to struggle for what was meaningful, and to this day it is in the cities where the struggle is the most intense.

Our last interchange was when I came to Detroit. Jimmy was ill and could not come to the program that night. But when I got to the house, he immediately embraced me with one hand—and with the other gave me three pages of questions that had to be resolved if we were going to make this an intelligent and decent society.

Reading his thoughts and propositions about the questions, I came across the concept that Racism as we had used it in our struggle was no longer valid, was indeed a very small designation of what the problems were. We needed to enlarge our frame of reference. Our Struggle could be meaningful only if it was a struggle in which everybody was fought *for* instead of fought *over;* nobody was any greater or any less than anyone else. The struggle in its purest sense had to be focused on elevating the lives of all the people. I began to understand what steps we must take if indeed we are to get from here to the twenty-first century. Once again James had given me an assignment, had given me insight, had given me comfort, had opened my mind and my heart, and all the avenues into my being were flooded with intelligence and understanding in the simplest, most direct way. I was born again.

Here today in his presence and his absence, as I share with you not only recollections of things past but an awareness that in a most profound way he is with us now and that in the most profound way he will be with us as we go into the battle, I am enheartened, I am encouraged, and I know that there is a victory. And although I may not see what I mean by "the victory" with my own eyes, my brothers, my sisters, and my children will indeed see it, and that makes the struggle worthwhile.

I have often thought that we of this age suffer from the arrogance of the nobility of our convictions. We truly believe that it is our responsibility to change the world, to change it completely for the benefit of all humankind. We set up institutions and instrumentalities and activities toward that end, fully expecting that one day the flag of oppression will fall and the flag of Brotherhood, Peace, and Justice will before our eyes be lifted to the skies.

We find from experience that the time is longer than we thought, that we may not have been the chosen generation to see the moment of victory. But perhaps our responsibility is to do the best we can to further the cause, fully understanding that although we may not see it in person, it will come to pass—to share with Shelley that we will "hope until hope itself creates from its own wreck the thing it contemplates."

I cannot stand before you without sharing my joy. I feel tears in my eyes, not necessarily of sorrow; but tears of transformation, tears of change—those tears that come to the human heart when once again, through Jimmy's grace and thought and goodness, I am given the privilege to be born again.

# LETTERS

*How do you fight that feeling of helplessness, of worth-*
*lessness, of drift? You get busy, you find something to*
*do—one thing, one small thing that points in the right*
*direction—and you do it. You try and network with*
*other people who have adopted the same response.*

*Whatever the problems are, we must face them as*
*responsible individuals. They will not go away, they*
*will not solve themselves of their own momentum. The*
*remedies are not self-administered. Somebody has to*
*take responsibility. Somebody has to be there where the*
*buck is bound to stop. And in a democracy, it's not the*
*president, it is not the Supreme Court, it's not the Con-*
*gress, it's not the mayors, it's not the cops on the corner.*
*In a democracy, it is the citizens who have the control-*
*ling and the deciding interest and, therefore, the con-*
*trolling and deciding responsibility. If something is to*
*be done, it is up to us either to do it ourselves or see to it*
*that it is done.*

*—Address to the Detroit Youth*
*Summer Program, 1988*

# TO WILLIAM PATTERSON

*February 1, 1964*

R.D.: *William Patterson was a civil rights attorney, activist, and longtime leader in the American Communist Party. We shared many struggles with Pat and his wife and colleague, Louise—from the fight to restore Paul Robeson's passport to the Committee to Free Angela Davis. Over the years, Pat and Louise became dear friends.*

Dear Pat,

This is a letter written out of some degree of anger, part of which I direct at you and part at myself. However, it is much more than a personal letter: it is to some degree a position paper in which I will attempt to clarify my relations with certain forces involved in the Negro Struggle, and to rearrange those relations in light of what I believe to be the truth.

Soon we will have had our Memorial to Dr. Du Bois, and we will then be faced with deciding what to do with what we have started. Already certain suggestions have been made as to what would be most fitting in the way of permanent commemoration of this, the greatest mind of the twentieth century. Something should be done. But I want no part of either deciding what that something is, or of serving to put that something into motion. My experience up to this time with the Memorial Committee leads me to forecast an internecine hassle between the forces of the Left and the Negro people over the hallowed bones of this genius, and I want no part of it.

The Left will tend to look upon Dr. Du Bois as theirs because his search for objective truth, as you say, led him finally to embrace the Party as his own. The Negro people will look upon the doctor as theirs because he was from beginning to end a Negro. The conflict between these points of view will probably be conducted in such a manner as to cast discredit upon both, and wind up insulting the man whom we both should join to honor.

You will object, and quite rightly, that I pose what is merely a difference between two entities as if there were a permanent ineradicable conflict, and that one could not therefore belong to one and to the other at the same time. And I will sustain your objection after I explain that I pose the question in this manner merely the better to examine it. Let me begin by pointing out what is of course obvious to all: the interests and objectives of the Left do not always and at every point coincide with those of the Negro people, especially in the short and immediate view.

(I move, in order to make my own arguments sound less insufferable, to strike all references to the "Negro people" and replace the phrase with "Negro Struggle.")

You will agree that the Left, per se, has a structure, philosophy, a strategy, a leadership, and a loyalty quite separate and distinct from the structure, philosophy, strategy, leadership, and loyalty of the Negro Struggle. It is possible, as has happened elsewhere, that ultimately the two might melt into each other and become indistinguishable, but that is a very remote possibility. At the present time the Negro people are in the vanguard of the forces working for change in this country, and though they could hardly have come to this place at this time without the past help and tutelage of the Left, that tutelage is over; and while the Negro people are properly grateful for past favors, what they need at this moment is, like an adolescent, to break away from the Great White Papa on all levels and in all areas, and to come to some sense of our own separate manhood and identity. The Negro people need desperately at this moment to feel that their struggle and their interests are paramount, not to be made subordinate to any view of the world that does not come and say "Amen" to that desire, no matter how childish the desire, or how correct and logical any worldview may be. I go to this inordinate length merely to state that the natural and normal differences between the two parties can and will lead to conflict in the areas of choice. I do that in order to state that when such a choice arises, I will as an individual categorically choose a "nationalist" point of view.

I arrive at this determination both from reflection upon the nature of the struggle in which we are involved, and more immediately from my own recent experiences with the formation of the Du Bois Memorial Committee. Let us review that formation from my point of view, however small, selfish, and possibly misguided that may be. I will deal in personalities because our relationship in the past will sustain it, and because I cannot otherwise defend my anger both at you and myself. But before it is alleged that I am being devious—that I am using a sudden and spurious newfound dedication to "my people" as a smoke screen behind which I can sneak out of the struggle, abandon commitment, and make myself "acceptable" in order to command a larger crumb from the tables of Television and the Movies—let me offer my rebuttal. I did not hesitate to initiate the fight to help Mr. Robeson secure a passport in my union, nor did I turn tail and run when the Un-American Committee had me up for that action; I did not hesitate to speak out for the Rosenbergs; I did not hesitate to openly help organize a reception for Mr. Robeson when he had his concert at Carnegie; I did not hesitate to co-sign an ad in the *New York Post* by the Fair Play for Cuba Committee, asking my country not to invade Cuba, though there was pressure to make me withdraw; I did not hesitate to appear on a program for CORE in Scarsdale when the affair was picketed because Pete Seeger was on the program and most other performers and speakers had withdrawn; I did not hesitate to openly invite Dr. Du Bois to be my guest at the opening of *Purlie Victorious;* I did not hesitate to accept an invitation for cocktails at the Hungarian Embassy. I did not hesitate to write a sketch and openly accept credit for it, at the request of Soviet-American Friendship (I forget the exact name, but Mr. Morford is its head). Nor in the future, when my usefulness to my own people as a small symbol of something in which they—as Negroes—can take pride is at stake, will I hesitate.

But, this "usefulness to my own people as a small symbol of something in which they can establish ownership and take pride" is of great and overriding importance to me. And here we come close to the angry end of our bone of contention. For, if the powers that be, who are always looking for a weapon with which to disrupt the Negro people, were to attack me as being a "willing, or unwitting, tool of the Communist conspiracy," and could document their charges with certain aspects of the formation of the Du Bois Memorial Committee, which—innocent and even honorable as you and I know them to be—they could possibly hurl quite a distraction into the midst of the Negro camp. And we would all wind up fighting amongst ourselves and thereby doing untold damage to that Unity of the Negro People so essential to any progress we can make. Let me reaffirm: the facts themselves are not even worthy of note or mention, but the use to which the facts can be put is most damnable, as you yourself well know. Already there are good people—strong people, who understand all—who accuse me of risking too much in this venture, and they base their criticism on the belief that the Left has learned nothing from its past. And especially with relations to Mr. Robeson, about whom there is still some anger, even from some segment of the Left.

I do not agree that the Left took advantage of Paul or misguided him: he was and is a grown man capable of making his own decisions, and I am sure he did. But look: let us discuss Mr. Robeson a moment, since he is key to so much of what I feel and to what I intend to do, and not to do in the future. In his book *Here I Stand,* he says:

> I sense a growing impatience (among our people) with petty ways of thinking and doing things. I see a rising resentment against control of our affairs by white people, regardless of whether that domination is expressed by the blunt orders of political bosses or more discreetly by the "advice" of white liberals, which must be heeded or else.

I quote you this passage because it defines very clearly the only "black nationalism" to which I subscribe, and it certainly comes from an internationalist and a humanist, if ever there was one.

But, more to the point, he says further:

> . . . I advocate a unity based upon our common viewpoint as Negroes, a nonpartisan unity, a unity in which we subordinate all that divides us, a unity which excludes no one, a unity in which no faction or group is permitted to impose its particular outlook on others. A unified leadership of a unified movement means that people of all political views—conservatives, liberals, and radicals—must be represented therein. Let there be but one requirement made without exception: that Negro leadership, and every man and woman in that leadership, place the interests of our people, and the struggle for those interests, above all else.

I personally believe that Mr. Robeson meant that, in any conflict of interest between dedication to the Negro people and their interests, and dedication to any other interest, however noble or worthy, or international or humanist it was, the true Negro leader would have to choose the interest of his people. If you assume, as I do, that such a unity is not only necessary, but possible, can you not also understand my assumption that there was a time when the only man who could have wrought such a unity was Mr. Robeson himself? And if Paul was the only man with both the understanding and power to do what was not only necessary, but possible, is it not great injury to us that circumstances made it impossible for him to do it? No matter what those circumstances were, and how important it was that he fight against them with all his strength and courage? Granted Paul was at a disadvantage, having been domiciled overseas during the crucial 12 years before World War II, and to some degree personally removed from the immediacies of the Negro Struggle; still, how wonderful if he and the Left had made a different analysis of the situation. If his value to the Negro people as a man and a symbol around which they could unify themselves could have been kept in the fore, and nothing attempted or done to in any way impair that relationship. If all other areas of identification had been deliberately suppressed or retarded until he had solidly and securely taken his natural place at the head of his people, and had consequently established a mass base of "black power," from which he could operate as Martin King was able to operate in Montgomery.

Unfortunately the decisive battle was fought around the narrow issue of a passport and a right to travel, which could hardly arouse a mass concern among his people as long as the powers that be could say that what he was fighting for was only "a Communist's right to travel." Granted, the right to travel by anybody—Communist or not—is an important one. Still, for Paul to take the lead in that fight could be made to seem as if he was struggling like hell not for his people, but for the right to get the hell away from them! You know different, I know different. But given the nature of mass communication and the devastating effectiveness of McCarthyism at alienating the American people, Negroes included, as a whole from the Communists, and given the Left's complete understanding that it was at a tremendous disadvantage, instead of keeping Paul as a major weapon in the front lines, knowing that the masses could not be brought up in time to effect his rescue, would it not have been strategically wiser to have saved him, to have kept him in reserve for use at a later date?

I am of course speaking entirely from unsupported supposition, and my analysis quite possibly departs from reality at all points. But surely the fact that this man was prevented from taking his place as our symbolic father and possible leader was disastrous from the Negro point of view. I pause to emphasize that I do not accuse the Left of ill intentions, but only of gross ineptness. In describing what happened in this case, and judging it solely from its effect on the Negro people, I can only use somebody's phrase: it was worse than a crime, it was a blunder. Why a blunder? Because the most truly revolutionary force in the country today is the Negro people, who, together with whatever allies they can scrape up, might possibly save us all, Left wing included. And to have provided the Negro people with a rallying cry and a unifying symbol—even at the expense of the Left—was historically more important than to have done the same service for the Left at the expense of the Negro people. And this came about primarily because I do not believe the Left has ever truly understood the inside of what it means to be black. Of course, this was not universal, and certainly those of you who are yourselves Negro understood it then, and understand it now. But I do not believe your voices were ever strong enough—or independent enough in the councils of the Left—to have made the necessary difference.

But back to the formation of the Du Bois Committee and my objections to some of its aspects. When you called me, just before I went to California, broaching the idea of some kind of memorial, I felt obliged to go along, because I think the doctor worthy of it, because I had been the one to mention him first at Washington, and most importantly, I felt that something should be done to restore the doctor to his rightful place as the keystone of the Negro Struggle in this country. But before I could talk to you at all, I had to leave.

During my absence, work was done to get the project off the ground. A meeting was called and a letter sent out over my name as the initiator. I have since discovered that Dorothy did ask Ruby if in her opinion it would be all right to send such a letter. Yet, nobody had taken the trouble to get my *direct* consent, or bothered themselves to find out if I could serve.

When I returned I was immediately swamped in more activity than I could manage: getting on an off-B'way show, where I had to function both as producer and performer; trying to save *Gone Are the Days,* which was dying at the box office, in addition to finding myself all of a sudden, in some small demand on TV, etc., not to mention my efforts with the Artist Association for Freedom, which was trying to organize a No Shopping for Xmas Campaign. I could not make the first meeting, so busy was I—but managed somehow to emerge as chairman of the committee. Although I was extremely busy, I didn't mind too much because when I have managed some affair for the civil rights organizations, they take care to spare me of as much detail as possible. Somebody is assigned to answer the phone and make the arrangements and pull the whole thing together, keeping me informed as they go along. Knowing you and Louise to be good and personal friends of mine, I just knew that the same kind of organization would be forthcoming. It was only when I used to look up every night after the show and see Louise, or Abbot, or Dorothy, that I got the truly appalling picture: for all intents and purposes, the whole thing was going to rest, every jot and tittle of it, on my unsolicited shoulders.

And it is at this point that my case against myself becomes damning: I gave Louise some very whiny, hurt, and bedraggled pleas for help when I saw her; I complained that a TV script bearing my name was not really mine, because I had not had the TIME to finish it. I was hoping she would get the message: *For God's sakes, HELP! Louise, I'm much too busy to do justice to this project.* But being basically a rather craven sort of coward in matters of personal morality, I chickened out. I never spoke up overtly, except to insist on a meeting with you, the object of which was to have been to let you know that I wouldn't mind being a part of the program, but that I could not assume any other responsibility. But I was too busy myself ever to come and talk to you. You will agree that I have a basic right to kick myself in my own behind for being too cowardly to confess that I was biting off more than I could chew.

But I knew that February was a long way away, so I stalled. In addition, I had some good friends of mine who were also Du Bois lovers on the committee, and I thought that, through them, maybe I could work it. But then a very delicate situation arose. In discussions about the first meeting, which I could not attend, I gathered that the project was in danger—"leftist dominated." In other words, a conflict of interests among people honestly drawn together by their love of Dr. Du Bois was already with us. These friends had two strong feelings: that if the committee were openly shown to be "leftist dominated," I stood a chance of getting hurt and of spoiling my own chances just when good things were beginning to happen to me—and through me, to all the other Negro performers who had been trying for years to get into TV and motion pictures. They felt that if I allowed myself to be knocked off, as had been done to so many people in the past for "leftist affiliations," I would spoil things in this very delicate area for too many others. And since Mr. Charlie didn't want us on TV anyhow, it would be doing the cause a grave disservice to leave myself open to possible red-baiting. I did not totally buy this theory, although there is more than a grain of truth in it.

They felt, in addition, that if I were knocked out and branded, that I would also do a disservice to the broader Negro Struggle, whose elements had begun more and more to identify Ruby and myself as belonging to the Negro people in a sense that no other artists did. Also that a left-wing dominated salute in which the Left would get up and celebrate the fact that THEY were the one and only heirs of Dr. Du Bois would upset whatever plans we might have to reclaim him for the Negro Struggle. They argued that the Left had chosen me because I could possibly muster up a broader-based popular support than anybody else, but would use the evening to make its own points at the expense of everybody else's. This, mind you, not from malice or ill intent, but because they didn't know any better.

These arguments did not rest lightly with me, since they came from people we both know and respect, and since I, too, have been deeply upset about many aspects of the Robeson Affair. And, to tell the truth, though I could understand and support the right of the Left to hold its own sectarian salute to the doctor in honor of the fact that his long search for objective truth had at last led him into the fold, the fact that the doctor had at last opted for an open embrace of the Communist Party meant nothing to me personally.

I felt, rather, that the times called for Dr. Du Bois to be restored as the guiding light of the Negro Struggle both in this country and in Africa. And I thought that if I could get the support and sponsorship of the six Negro civil rights leaders in a salute to Dr. Du Bois, it would be a most worthwhile thing. I felt so strongly about this that I insisted that the Left not participate either in the sponsorship or in the performance of the program. I did this deliberately because I valued the support of a Martin Luther King, and a Roy Wilkins much more highly in this instance than that of a Ben Davis or a William Patterson. These men, however ineptly, represent black power-in-being, and their embracing of Dr. Du Bois could open the way for the people they represented to embrace him. And once this happened, all the wealth of Du Bois, the treasury of his passion and his thought, would be available to the Negro people. Ben and Pat, however much closer they were to the doctor in thought and feeling, do not represent this black power. So I did not hesitate to ask them to step aside.

Yet, if the possibility of advocacy, direct or indirect, was to be denied to the Left, it must also be denied to those who might be moved to give the doctor a good cleaning by apologizing for him. I thought to solve this problem by permitting no one to speak for the doctor but himself: to dramatize certain important segments of his own words, and pass them on, red hot, to the people gathered at Carnegie Hall. I knew of course that I did not have the time to do such a dramatization, yet who else was there?

Though the Left had agreed to some of my conditions about initiating sponsors, etc., it did not, and possibly could not, agree to all. It was the Left I have reason to believe who had put up the money (I was not consulted on this) with which to secure the hall. And he who pays the piper calls the tune. The Left has a rightful claim to the doctor and is fearful lest that claim go unrecognized. The "nationalists" feel slighted, first in that the doctor left his papers to a white man, and sent for a white man to eulogize his remains. They fear the Left is out to control the program, which to some degree it is, and that what the doctor means or can mean to the Negro people will be left out, or dragged in last as usual. This split has debilitated work on every level, making it even more necessary that I—who have less and less time to spare—should mediate, beg, cajole, explain, soothe, and patch up, and take into my own hands more and more of the activities. To publicize the affair has become a main function for me, taking up more and more time that I have less and less of.

And now, Pat, we meet, you and I. And through you, I get to know the feelings and wishes of the Left, for whom I find myself working, without once having been asked. I accept their rejection of Miss Price. I accept their rejection of Jimmie McDonald, whom I had begged to come in and try and do for me many of the things I had no time to do for myself. And I note the fact that Dorothy made no complaint to me, who had put Jimmie there, but to you, the real source of power and authority in the project. (I do not fault Dorothy one whit in this. She's tops in my book.) I accept the Left's insistence on inspecting the script in order to make sure it is getting what it pays for. I draw this conclusion from the fact that the Left already knows that I am a writer of skill, and that I can write very well in the dramatic reading format. So the only logical reason for this insistence is to make sure of the content.

I did not start out to write a script about Dr. Du Bois for the Left, and yet I am doing so. I did not start out to head a committee and to attend to long and boring details about pricing the balcony, or whether or not we need name entertainers to get people to come to a memorial to the doctor (for if that be the case, how will we know whether people came to salute Dr. Du Bois, or Lena Horne?), and yet I am doing so. I did not start out intending to have to drop everything and come running to you to get the latest thinking on the project from those who foot the bill. And yet I am doing it. Why?

Partially because somebody has to. I have, and to some degree on the strength of my name alone, gotten a broader spectrum of sponsors for the salute than anybody else could. And that is a positive good. Partially because the doctor is worth all the trouble it takes to try and get him back to his own. (Although I know that the doctor himself would hardly put up for one minute with the foolishness of our childish quarrel over his honored bones. The doctor saved himself, and I doubt if he ever got maneuvered by his own weaknesses into heading many committees. He was too busy doing what was important: thinking! No man can live so long and accomplish so much who does not have the power to say *No!* except to the deepest needs of his own nature. I live for the day when I will have balls enough to do likewise.) Partially because my respect for you and Louise is a profound one, and will continue so although our relations have changed. Partially out of ego satisfaction. Everybody likes to feel that he, and he alone, is the only man who can do what needs to be done. I am no exception in this folly. But this experience has cured me, I think. And partially because I lack the ability to exercise independent judgment when called upon by my friends. Unlike the good doctor, I cannot say NO! But when the time comes to organize the next step AFTER Carnegie Hall, I intend to give it a good try.

It is my intention to call a halt to my outside activities and concentrate more on becoming as good a playwright as I can. I know that the contribution I make to the struggle this way will be much more profound than any made in any other manner. This does not mean that I will withdraw from the struggle. It merely means I intend to say No! at my own discretion until I am convinced that another form of attack is needed from me. (Think of what it might have meant if Louis Burnham could have learned to say no. Do you remember the doctor's comments on Louis?) I have worked hard to establish a center of belongingness with my people at whatever level they are, and to do nothing, don't give a damn what, to upset or jeopardize that relationship. And if you think being identified with the Left is of no consequence, how would you explain that two of the men who understand the struggle more than any of its current leaders, and who have themselves talent for mass leadership—how do you explain that these men, for whatever reason—that Pat and Ben, for whatever reason, are not at the center of that struggle?

You may say that it is of more importance that these men hold their loyalty to the Left above all others, since the interests of the Left and of the Negro people are bound at some time to coincide, and that the greatest service they can perform for their people is to hold aloft the banner of internationalism and humanism and peace, at the expense of all that would demand a less inclusive view of the world. That the highest loyalty is always to objective truth, and that objective truth can be no respecter of person, or creed, or of color. But, Gentlemen, are you not disturbed that the Socialist Camp, which to millions is in itself the embodiment of the highest objective truth, has allowed itself to be split into hostile factions, along what appear to be racial lines? Can you, from the top of your knowledge to the bottom of your heart, swear that the sentiments I express in this letter are totally unrelated to that tragic fact?

When you shall bring these scrambled, hasty thoughts to judgment, and have given them the benefit of your dialectical wisdom, and conclude that I am wrong in every point, forget not that I express what many of my brothers in and out of the arts feel. And men are prone to act upon their feelings, even if those feelings are wrongly arrived at.

Bertolt Brecht (and think of what he did for the cause

purely as a playwright) has passed on the following bit of advice to writers:

> Nowadays anyone who wishes to combat lies and ignorance and to write the truth must overcome at least five difficulties. He must have the courage to write the truth when truth is everywhere opposed; the keenness to recognize it although it is everywhere concealed; the skill to manipulate it as a weapon; the judgment to select those in whose hands it will be effective; and the cunning to spread the truth among such persons.

And in support of his first point, the one about courage, he had this to add:

> And it also takes courage to tell the truth about oneself, about one's own defeat. Many of the persecuted lose their capacity for seeing their own mistakes: It seems to them that the persecution itself is the greatest injustice. The persecutors are wicked simply because they persecute; the persecuted suffer because of their goodness. But—this goodness has been beaten!, defeated!, suppressed!; it was therefore a weak goodness, a bad, indefensible, unreliable goodness. For it will not do to grant that goodness must be weak as rain must be wet. *It takes courage to say that the good were defeated not because they were good, but because they were weak.* *

---

*From "Writing the Truth: Five Difficulties" by Bertolt Brecht, translated by Richard Winston, in *Art in Action: Twice a Year 1938–1948*, 10th Anniversary Issue (New York: Twice a Year Press, 1948).

I join Mr. Brecht in offering this advice to the American Left: that if it was defeated, it was not because it was good, but because it was weak. And that it was weak precisely because it insisted, like General Motors, that what was good for the Party was good for the Negro people. I do not believe this to be necessarily so. The thought comes closer to the truth if you turn it around. If Socialism comes to this country, and that may well be her only hope of salvation, it may well be that the Negroes will create it. And the Socialism the Negro people embrace will be, essentially, Negro Socialism, bidding fair to take its place beside Russian Socialism, and Chinese Socialism, and Yugoslavian, and African Socialism, etc. And unless the Left can learn to live with the fact that all roads to Socialism must begin as struggles for nationalism, separate but equal, and that Negro Socialism is the only possibility before us in America, you run the risk of consigning yourselves to eventual irrelevancy, an anachronism which perished because it could not cope with the change it had itself helped to bring about.

Suppose my wild-eyed theory is correct: that the true carrier of change in this country is in the Negro Struggle rather than the Left, and that if the Left is to remain viable and relevant it must run like hell to catch up with that revolutionary force—suppose, I say, these things are demanded by an objective reading of the truth. Do you think the Left, as it is now constituted, could humble itself to the point of playing second fiddle, even for its own survival, to a revolution led by Negroes? If history has called upon us—old, black, miserable, laughed at, despised US—to lead in the next stage of this country's development, could the Left bring itself to happily join in without wanting or needing to call the shots?

Enough of irrelevant chatter. Let me close with a parable: There was once, in the forefront of the Struggle, a Vanguard with an international point of view from which it was able to provide guidance and leadership to the main body of troops marching towards the Promised Land. All went well until the Vanguard, so excited in what it thought to be a glimpse of that land, allowed itself to be surrounded, cut off, and isolated from the main body of troops. The main body, deprived of guidance and a chance to get its international bearings from the Vanguard, had to fall back on its own narrow, sectarian, nationalistic point of view in order to protect itself and to survive. The Vanguard still possesses a high vantage from which it can look over into the Promised Land and describe all the wonders therein. It shouts its delights and its instructions back to the main troops, but there is so much interference and jamming that the main body cannot hear the instructions, and continues to stumble along blindly, desperately in need of guidance, but not being sufficiently in touch with the Vanguard to get it. The situation worsens. The Vanguard on the high spot is a sitting duck for snipers and mortar fire. It becomes so busy defending itself and the narrow height it occupies that it cannot send instructions back. Finally, under pressure of events, the main body abandons hope of ever hearing from the Vanguard. It blindly starts forward on its own tack, not knowing where it is going, but knowing that it must go. It drifts further and further from the Vanguard, which is now decimated and greatly weakened from having had to cling to such an exposed position, instead of having found a way back. Now the two are almost entirely out of contact. The Vanguard is still in possession of the Master Plan, but the main body has long since moved out of earshot. The only hope now is that the main body will, by sheer luck and blind instinct, still manage somehow to stumble in the right direction and finally reach the Promised Land. But there is no guarantee, only hope.

You, and Ben, and Louise and the others are with the Vanguard, Pat. You have occupied a high place under the most withering fire. One by one, you have watched your comrades fall off, or get knocked off; you have shouted your instructions, but the crowd is too far away to hear you. All you have left is your own knowledge that yonder, just over the high mountain, is the place we all must get to. It is there, and it is real, and you can see it with your own eyes—that, and the hope that the main body of troops from which you have too long been cut off, will somehow find the right way without you. You could come down, perhaps, and fight your way back to the main body, but that would mean deserting your friends, and abandoning the high place for which you paid with your blood. You prefer to stay where history has placed you, knowing of the real possibility that the tide of battle swirling below might bring the main troops back within earshot some time in the future. There you are in splendid isolation, and I salute you for your bravery.

But I choose to stay with the main troops, even in this the month of their blindness. I choose to try and form another Vanguard, one which will not dare so high a peak again, and will therefore sacrifice a great deal of its international point of view. One which will not stray too far from the main body, because it has learned from your example the real meaning of Che Guevara's dictum in *Guerrilla Warfare: "The first duty of a guerrilla fighter is to survive!"* (I mean survive as a guerrilla fighter.)

Or what I choose to call the Paul Robeson Law: Never stick your neck out further than your feet are planted deep in the people—there are too many people just waiting to chop it off.

I count on your discretion to reserve this letter for only the proper eyes.

Yours for Peace and Friendship,
Ossie Davis

# TO ROGER PRICE*

~

*March 11, 1965*

R.D.: *Ossie and I argued about the end of this letter, which I felt did a disservice to the many black men we both admired—men like John Henrik Clarke, and like Ossie's own father, who never held their tongues or hesitated to stand by their convictions.*

O.D.: *Many people, not understanding who Malcolm really was and what he meant to black folk, were surprised that I should speak at his funeral . . .*

Dear Roger:

You are not the only person curious to know why I would eulogize a man like Malcolm X. Many who know and respect me have written letters. Of these letters, I am proudest of those from a sixth grade class of young white boys and girls who asked me to explain. I appreciate your giving me this chance to do so.

You may anticipate my defense somewhat by considering the following fact: no Negro has yet asked me that question.

---

*The editor of *Grump* magazine, Price went on to create the television series *The Tomorrow People* and *You Can't Do That on Television*. This letter appeared as an article (titled "On Malcolm X") in the July 1965 edition of *Grump*.

(My pastor in Grace Baptist Church where I teach Sunday School preached a sermon about Malcolm in which he called him a "giant in a sick world.") Every one of the many letters I got from my own people lauded Malcolm as a man, and commended me for having spoken at his funeral.

At the same time—and this is important—most all of them took special pains to disagree with much or all of what Malcolm said and what he stood for. That is, with one singing exception: they all, every last, black, glory-hugging one of them, knew that Malcolm—whatever else he was or was not—*Malcolm was a man!*

White folks do not need anybody to remind them that they are men. We do! This was his one incontrovertible benefit to his people.

Protocol and common sense require that Negroes stand back and let the white man speak up for us, defend us, and lead us from behind the scene in our fight. This is the essence of Negro Politics. But Malcolm said to hell with that! Get up off your knees and fight your own battles. That's the way to win back your self-respect. That's the way to make the white man respect you. And if he won't let you live like a man, he certainly can't keep you from dying like one!

Malcolm, as you can see, was refreshing excitement: he scared the hell out of the rest of us, bred as we are to caution, to hypocrisy in the presence of white folks, to the smile that never fades. Malcolm knew that every white man in America profits directly or indirectly from his position vis-à-vis Negroes, profits from racism even though he may not practice it or believe in it.

He also knew that every Negro who did not challenge on

the spot every instance of racism, overt or covert, committed against him and his people, who chose instead to swallow his spit and go on smiling, was an Uncle Tom and a traitor, without balls or guts, or any other commonly accepted aspects of manhood!

Now, we knew all these things as well as Malcolm did, but we also knew what happened to people who stick their necks out and say them. And if all the lies we tell ourselves by way of extenuation were put into print, it would constitute one of the great chapters in the history of Man's justifiable cowardice in the face of other men.

But Malcolm kept snatching our lies away. He kept shouting the painful truth we whites and blacks did not want to hear. And he wouldn't stop for love nor money.

You can imagine what a howling, shocking nuisance this man was to both Negroes and whites. Once Malcolm fastened on you, you could not escape. He was one of the most fascinating and charming men I have ever met, and never hesitated to take his attractiveness and beat you to death with it. Yet his irritation, though painful to us, was most salutary. He would make you angry as hell, but he would also make you proud. It was impossible to remain defensive and apologetic about being a Negro in his presence. He wouldn't let you. And you always left his presence with the sneaky suspicion that maybe, after all, you *were* a man.

But in explaining Malcolm, let me take care not to explain him away. He had been a criminal, an addict, a pimp, and a prisoner; a racist, and a hater, he had really believed the white man was a devil. But all this had changed. Two days before his death, in commenting to Gordon Parks about his past life, he said: "That was a mad scene. The sickness and madness of those days! I'm glad to be free of them."

And Malcolm was free. No one who knew him before and after his trip to Mecca could doubt that he had completely abandoned racism, separatism, and hatred. But he had not abandoned his shock-effect statements, his bristling agitation for immediate freedom in this country not only for blacks, but for everybody.

And most of all, in the area of race relations, he still delighted in twisting the white man's tail, and in making Uncle Toms, compromisers, and accommodationists—I deliberately include myself—thoroughly ashamed of the urbane and smiling hypocrisy we practice merely to exist in a world whose values we both envy and despise.

But even had Malcolm not changed, he would still have been a relevant figure on the American scene, standing in relation as he does to the "responsible" Civil Rights leaders, just about where John Brown stood in relation to the "responsible" Abolitionist in the fight against slavery. Almost all disagreed with Brown's mad and fanatical tactics, which led him foolishly to attack a Federal arsenal at Harpers Ferry, to lose two sons there, and later to be hanged for treason. Yet today the world, and especially the Negro people, proclaim Brown not a traitor, but a hero and a martyr in a noble cause. So in the future, I will not be surprised if men come to see that Malcolm X was, within his own limitations and in his own inimitable style, also a martyr in that cause. But there is much controversy still about this most controversial American, and I am content to wait for history to make the final decision.

But in personal judgment, there is no appeal from instinct. I knew the man personally, and however much I disagreed with him, I never doubted that Malcolm X, even when he was wrong, was always that rarest thing in the world among us Negroes: a true man. And if, to protect my relations with the many good white folks who make it possible for me to earn a fairly good living in the entertainment industry, I was too chicken, too cautious, to admit that fact when he was alive, I thought at least that now, when all the white folks are safe from him at last, I could be honest with myself enough to lift my hat for one final salute to that brave, black, ironic gallantry, which was his style and hallmark, that shocking ZING of fire-and-be-damned-to-you, so absolutely absent in every other Negro man I know, which brought him, too soon, to his death.

# TO READERS' FORUM

Freedomways, *First Quarter 1967*

In February of 1966, *Liberator*—a magazine on whose advisory board I sat—published an article, "Semitism in the Black Ghetto" by Eddie Ellis, which I felt went beyond the bounds of black nationalism. I felt it was racist and said so to the editor, a man whom I still respect, Dan Watts. But "Semitism in the Black Ghetto" blows it for me, but good, and but definitely. This is where I get off!

If Mr. Ellis has proof of the wild and unsupported contentions that he made (how dare he charge that W.E.B. Du Bois was "used" by "Zionists" to attack Marcus Garvey?), where is that proof? Jews are active in civil rights; Jews do have policy-making positions in civil rights organizations; Jewish philanthropies were, and still are, influential in Negro affairs. But is this due to their "evil cunning"—or to our weaknesses? Mr. Ellis says all these activities are part of a Zionist plan to make Negroes scapegoats instead of themselves. But where the hell is the proof? Mr. Ellis doesn't even offer us a "protocols of Zion"!

We could argue for years about what Jews have done *to* and *for* Negroes in this country; and whether what has been done has resulted in good or bad for the Negro people. But who in his right mind can argue that that which was done and is being done by Jews in particular, whether good or bad, is part of a gigantic plot to dupe and take advantage of Negroes; a deliberate, agreed-upon "Zionist," "Jewish Community," "Semitic" plot against Negroes?

Where is that proof?

I am not sentimental about Jews, Negroes, or anybody else. And I am not grateful. People should fight for freedom because they believe in freedom. I know Jews who do, and I know Jews who don't; I know Negroes who do, and I know Negroes who don't. A man should fight for what he believes in—and the fact that he fights is his reward. I owe him nothing.

Harlem is a deprived and exploited community, but are Jews the only ones who profit from this exploitation? No! Are Jews the ones who profit *most* by this exploitation? I strongly doubt it. (Mr. Ellis would have done us all a favor if he had conducted a survey to determine who, in fact, really owns Harlem.)

Whatever Jews are guilty of exploiting Harlem are not guilty because they are Jews, but because—along with many Catholics, Protestants, Negro and white—they are exploiters. In a war against all exploiters whomsoever, I am an ally. But Mr. Ellis seems to be calling for a war against Jews. If that is the case, I am an enemy.

You see, I consider myself a Black Nationalist, and proud to be one . . . but not a Black racist. And I consider the difference between them too fundamental for compromise.

*Black Nationalism* is as legitimate and honorable a vehicle of the black man's anguish as Irish nationalism was to the Irish, and Zionism to the Jews. But *Black racism* is no different from any other racism. I think few people will doubt my love and respect for our late Brother Malcolm X. I call your attention to an article in the *New York Times* by M.S. Handler, quoting a letter he had received abroad from Malcolm. In this letter Brother Malcolm specifically renounced racism and pledged himself to spend the rest of his life making up for the *racism* he had formerly preached. That Malcolm at last became wise enough to see racism as a vicious, destructive crime against the human spirit with most frightening implications; that he sharply set it apart from nationalism; that, above all, he set out to undo the harm he himself had done in formerly advocating black racism—is the measure of his personal integrity and his greatness as a man and as a leader.

The beauty of Brother Malcolm was that he was intelligent enough to grow away from past errors, and to stretch out his hands towards *truth* even if they shot him down for it. Malcolm X was a Black Nationalist in the true sense of the word. Can we who love him be less?

Ossie Davis
*New Rochelle, New York*

# TO JAY WOLF

*April 21, 1968*

R.D.: *Jay Wolf was our agent for many years and sensitive to our concerns as black actors. I understood his feelings about* The Slaves, *but Ossie and I always believed that the best way to influence a project is from the inside—especially when it involves your friends.*

Dear Jay,

Here is the letter I promised you concerning my current thoughts and feelings about *The Slaves*. You have always rather strongly advised me against it on the basis that the work was awkwardly conceived, and backward-looking in its attitude. (You even compared it to *Birth of a Nation*.) You have asked me, time after time—as has my wife, Ruby—why do this particular film on this particular subject at this particular time? And I have never fully answered you. I must do so now, for not only are you my agent, having as your assignment the protection of all interests—even from my own desires sometimes—but more importantly, because you are my friend.

First, I feel the "truth" about Uncle Tom, even as presented in the novel, has been perverted by the numerous melodramas that flooded the country for many years, and that it is from these distortions that we get our current concept of Tom. I also feel that Tom is a moral man, a good man, a religious man . . . and it is my firm belief that such a man can be shown—not as a prig, or a prude, or a masochistic self-demeaning slob, who goes around inviting the world to piss in his face—but as a man with balls and passion and courage, who—like Martin Luther King—is nobody's coward, but in reality the very quintessence of socially responsible bravery. Such a man could be a true nobleman, whom all who saw would be bound to respect and admire. I felt that the current concept of Uncle Tom—even as presented by Harriet Beecher Stowe—is that he is so good, and so kind, that he is ineffectual . . . that he is to be pitied, and therefore to be patronized. I felt that something should be done to correct that image. For too many good, sound Americans still feel that Negroes by and large are good, kind, and ineffectual . . . that they are people to be helped and pitied . . . and this is an attitude which still characterizes much of the White Liberal thinking about Negroes to this day; this is why they feel so threatened by Stokely and Rap and those who go around mouthing strange slogans like "Black Power." (Most whites who grieve over the tragic death of Dr. King do so because his devotion to nonviolence made him "holy" in their sight—and certainly nonviolence as a concept does not threaten them or their well-being. What they refuse to see is that King was a revolutionary, dedicated to the complete abolition and overthrow of the status quo, and that, in pursuit of his dream of the regeneration of the American Soul, a lot of them—good, white, compassionate people that they are—would wind up getting run over and hurt by that Revolution in which King firmly and irrevocably believed. King was committed to the day he died to nonviolence, but to nonviolence only as a means . . . a civilized means . . . a Christian means . . . a peaceful means by which to achieve completely revolutionary ends. And it was his ends, not necessarily his means, which are the true measure of his greatness. King was a revolutionary, reaching out for power with which to change society from top to bottom, that is what he was, and that was his greatness. This is what puts him in the same class as Malcolm and Stokely. He differed in tactics, in means, in his absolute devotion to nonviolence. But King knew that if nonviolence failed, then violence would take over. He knew that, violently or nonviolently, the American Revolution would someday be completed, even at the cost of much black and white blood and treasure. It is a terrible truth, but he faced it squarely, and tried to get America to face it. But the important thing is that King was no saint, putting his devotion to goodness and kindness above every consideration— he was no saint: he was a revolutionary! THAT is what he was, and that is his legacy to mankind.)

(Jesus was also no holy Joe, no do-gooder, no pious psalm singer—he, too, was a real revolutionary. And my personal appreciation of Jesus Christ is based, as is my devotion to Martin Luther King, upon that fact!)

Harriet Stowe's Uncle Tom was a good man, but his goodness was never made revolutionary. He measured his goodness by his own impulse to self-perfection, hoping that his moral example would light a flame which would change the inhuman heart of slavery. He failed, but in his failure he passed on the torch to others—mostly white. I thought a story in which Tom's goodness *was* made revolutionary, *did* finally become an active goodness that organized itself—and others—into active opposition to slavery, would be a good thing. I still think so. And this was, and still is, the basis for my willingness to be involved in such an "old hat" story as this. I thought Tom could be updated and made relevant to the current scene. Not by making him Stokely, nor even Martin Luther King, but by making him fight slavery as best he could, and finally learn not to trust in the goodness of white folks to save him, but to learn to rely upon himself and his black brothers in bondage to take matters into their own hands and attack slavery—even with force and violence—because he had come at last to learn that kindness and goodness in a master can never be relied on by the slave: the slave must rely on himself!

The various versions of the story as prepared by Herbert have moved, agonizingly slowly, towards this objective. John O. Killens has been of tremendous help. But I still feel that nobody has come to grips with Tom (now called Luke) in a manner that excites my acting appetite. To be brutally frank, it is only my respect and admiration for Herbert Biberman—especially his courageous and heartbreaking fight against McCarthyism—and my desire to see him recompensed for all his personal suffering in some way—it is these things that have kept me hanging on, hoping and praying that somebody would come up with a Tom (or a Luke) that I could play. This has not yet happened. And you tell me—as do others—to cut bait. Especially now, when the hunger is so great in the black community for a Hero they can admire and identify with, I am deeply concerned to do what satisfies my own people. I do not feel that Luke yet meets this test, and this is the deepest source of my dissatisfaction: the fear that black people who know me and trust me (and white people, too) would one day walk up to me after seeing it, and say: Ossie, you of all people, how could you do a part like that? You, who have openly fought with Hollywood for daring to film Nat Turner? You, who know how painful the whole subject of slavery is to the black psyche, how sick and tired we are of seeing our men pictured as ball-less saints instead of flesh and blood fighters?

Frankly, Jay, I would throw the whole thing over, except for the fact I still believe that such a character, truly and understandingly delineated (especially in conjunction with Jericho), would be a positive contribution. Also, I do desire to help Herbert in this project which has come to mean so much to him. Also, John O. Killens is one of my best friends. (It is not his fault if he came into the project very late, and that having come in as a writer, he still is a writer of novels—primarily—which is not the same as a writer of dramas. A novelist may merely describe a character and his actions and his feelings . . . a dramatist must dramatize them—a very great difference.) Also, would it be fair to turn my back on Herbert now, and let him come in with a film that would make him—of all people—the target of the deep and real outrage against all handling of Negro images in the black community?

I have tried to be as helpful as I know how. Have had many conferences, have submitted a seven-page letter of criticisms and suggestions, which both Herbert and John have accepted and appreciated. On the basis of some of the things I said, John has come up with much improvement in the story as it concerns Negro characters and their motivations. Still, where the character and actions and motives of Luke are concerned, the story still misses. I had thought that, while I am working out here, I would, once again, put my own writing aside—although I have sworn before almighty God I would not do that again—and write these sections of the story that dealt with Luke as I saw and felt them. But I haven't the time. Also, how can I assume prerogatives properly belonging to Herbert and John, and not myself?

I hope this letter will show you the depth of my problem, for I do not want you to think I am merely being Sancho to Herb's Quixote. I want this film to work; I want it to be something with which the whites could look to for a new understanding of how we got to where we are, and the blacks could look to for identity, and a new feeling of pride and respect in the discovery that black men did put up noble resistance to slavery, and that—most important of all—black men did come to a realization that if they wanted freedom, then as now, it is to themselves (not to their good masters, like Stillwell in the story, nor to their evil masters, like MacKay in the story, but to themselves, them DAMN BLACK SLAVES!) for their deliverance. Much of this is there now. But I still feel that Luke is far more pitiful than admirable. There is, to my mind, considerable work to be done. Can it be done before July first? I wonder.

Do me a favor. Ask Herb for a copy of the latest revised script, and show him this letter. It will save me having to write a separate one to him.

Believe me, Jay. I appreciate your concern for me, both as writer and actor. Your feeling about the "impossibly" small fee is well taken. But let me reiterate. Money was not, nor is, the main object here. I have a commitment to Herb which it would break my heart not to keep, even for half the money. What makes me unhappy is that I fear we will all come out of this—if we are not careful—as burning examples of the oldest-but-truest cliché in the world: The Road to Hell Is Paved with Good Intentions.

Sincerely,
Ossie

# TO SEYMOUR PECK*

June 26, 1972

R.D.: *Talk about fury as an actor! Nothing could ruin my day quite like finding out that a choice black role (when there were so few) was going to be played by a white actor. When such a grievance takes hold, it is comforting to know there's an outlet for frustrations. Ossie and I were big on writing letters. We used to keep lists of newspaper, radio, and television contacts for easy access. We wanted the children to know the importance of expressing their opinions. Sometimes it does make a difference—and you may even get your letter printed in the paper.*

Dear Sir:

I join my voice emphatically to those who feel it would be absolutely wrong for Tony Quinn to try to portray Henri Christophe in film, especially at this time when we black folks and other Third World people are fighting so hard to establish control over our identities. Tony is a great actor and I am happy to count him as a friend, and as an artist for whom I have the highest regard. But more than art is at issue here. And as a black man—fully aware that "black" in spite of its high

---

*Drama editor for the *New York Times*.

visibility is still too much distorted in American film, even by well-meaning whites—I must protest.

Sam Goldwyn, Jr., is a friend of mine, yet I did not hesitate to break with him over whether certain fictitious characters were truly and squarely black enough in the presentation in his forthcoming sequel to *Cotton Comes to Harlem*. How much more am I ready to say No! when a real black hero is about to be filmed. I would not consider playing the role of Benito Juarez even if I were asked. I love the man and he was certainly as great and as noble as Henri Christophe. But Juarez was a Mexican, and I know how proud Mexicans would have felt if a Mexican, perhaps Tony himself, had played that great hero instead of Paul Muni. I have yet to meet a Mexican who was flattered or inspired by Wallace Beery's leering portrayal of General Francisco Villa, and they might well have been had Tony played that revolutionary hero.

How many Mexican parents do you imagine really believed that their children would become better Mexicans by going to see Marlon Brando pretending to be Emiliano Zapata?

My black children need black heroes on which to model their behavior. Henri Christophe is an authentic black hero. Tony, for all my admiration of him as a man and as a talent, will do himself and my children a great disservice if he encourages them to believe that only a white man (and Tony is white to my children) is capable of portraying a black hero.

This is cultural emasculation, from which both Tony's people and mine have suffered too damn long. In the name of the millions of blacks who are desperately searching the screen and the Tube for some slight hint that we blacks, too, have had our giants in government and statesmanship as well as in sports and tap dancing—I vote a resounding NO!

Sincerely,
Ossie Davis

# TO MY COUNTRY

Los Angeles Times, *February 18, 2001*

*I've been to the mountaintop . . . and I've
seen the Promised Land.*
—MARTIN LUTHER KING, JR.

We African-Americans, no matter how stable or infirm
the national circumstance, have always kept our eyes,
our hopes, and our grip firmly on the Bill of Rights. It is our
passport, our spiritual identity, our right to occupancy, our
legal document of last resort—welcomed or not. For America,
our Step-Motherland, has always held us less dear than all the
rest—something less than love-hate, but certainly more than
bittersweet, has always stood between us. Still we are, by nature, God and law, a free people too; our rights, by struggle
bred, as constitutionally deep as all the rest. The trouble is,
though free, we are not equal. And so we often spend the mid-
night waiting for the other shoe to drop.

My people and I, good or bad, small or large, by ignorance
and jealousy are still detained. Too many blacks are still quar-
antined in the staging area just outside the mainstream. Can
we come in? Or will you be always needing an underdog to
complement your ethnic self-importance?

I hope not: I think not; just down is almost over, and time
is running out. Racial profiles, our blood-bought right to vote

(trashed in Florida), Amadou Diallo, Abner Louima—and how many more must Texas drag behind the cruel velocity of her contempt? Two hundred years and more, and you still doubt the loyalty of our citizenship?

Name me one war, one campaign, one battle fought in the name of freedom where we said no.

Life, liberty, and the pursuit of happiness. You hold—you say—these truths to be self-evident? Well, so do we. But cowardice, in the name of Jesus Christ, is not patriotism, and turning the other cheek is no longer an option we set before our children; we have become too American for that.

Lest we forget, what brought us here in the first place is not what brought you here. But we can modify the evil consequences. There is a basic good—projected and protected by the law—that America expects from all her patron lovers. But much depends on how we see—and where we set—the Promised Land.

The same Promised Land that Martin saw, and they killed him for it. But not before he took us all to the mountaintop, showed us the future just on the other side and guaranteed that someday we'd have possession too. But how long, Martin, how long?

Yes, Martin, on that last night in Memphis, with the politics of his clairvoyance, made the future much surer than the past. And so, in spite of the present haze and clouds of doubts and dragging feet, of hearty camouflage, smiling, but cold of hand, and saying, "No! I still discern the promise of America." And still remain a much committed man.

So, standing before you now, where Martin stood I say to

you in a raised voice: Tear down this wall! We are the mirror where America reads the health of all her principles. Our welfare is the test of this democracy. Or do you see us still the great American bane and afterthought? Does our history, in spite of Martin, still call in secret smirks and winks behind our backs for white and colored drinking fountains?

This subtle barricade between us, whatever it becomes, may yet see the break-up of this nation. Tear it down. Surely, if either of us could have built this thing we call America without the other's help, we would have done it long ago. The stone that holds us back and weighs us down requires a push from both our hands. Tear it down! This Bill of Rights, this holy orchestration, cannot be played if half the instruments choose to remain tone-deaf.

Then let us build America together, the people's one beloved and sure defense, ours as well as yours, shared equally among us all.

Like water fits the swimmer, like breathing fits the lungs, like seeing fits as far as the eye can see.

One nation, indivisible, at long, at last, America.

# AFTERWORD

*The gift that [Ruby and I] had was that there was a vision set before us and our people that we could see and understand and participate in. We had a focus from the time we set foot onstage up until this very day. In a sense, we always knew where we were going, we always knew why it was important to go there, and we always knew that in order to get there you had to make concessions, you had to duck sometimes but you always came back to true north, you always came back to the true course of what it was that we as a people—and as Ruby said, we as human beings—must attach ourselves to. We can't float through life. We can't be incidental or accidental. We must fix our gaze on a guiding star as soon as one comes upon the horizon, and once we have attached ourselves to that star we must keep our eyes on it and our hands on the plow. It is the consistency of the pursuit of the highest possible vision that you can find in front of you that gives you the constancy, that gives you the encouragement, that gives you the way to understand where you are and why it's important for you to do what you can do.*

—Interview with Tavis Smiley,
National Public Radio, November 2005

# THE BENEDICTION

~

*1961*

R.D.: *The idea was always to end this book with the closing mono-logue from* Purlie Victorious, *this proud, merry, soul-happy evoca-tion of blackness. After all, Ossie reasoned, why write an afterword when you've already got one handy? I like to think of it now as a final affirmation, a good-bye kiss from Ossie to all of us.*

Tonight, my friends, I find in being black a thing of beauty: a joy; a strength; a secret cup of gladness; a native land in neither time nor place—a native land in every Negro face! Be loyal to yourselves: your skin; your hair; your lips; your southern speech; your laughing kindness—are Negro kingdoms, vast as any other! Accept in full the sweetness of your blackness—not wishing to be red, nor white, nor yellow, nor any other race or face, but this. Farewell, my deep and Africanic brothers. Be brave; keep freedom in the family; do what you can for the white folks; and write me in care of the post office. Now, may the Constitution of the United States go with you; the Declaration of Independence stand by you; the Bill of Rights protect you; and the State Commission Against Discrimination keep the eyes of the law upon you henceforth, now and forever. Amen.